About Phonics Connection:

Welcome to Rainbow Bridge Publishing's Connection series. Like our Summer Bridge Activities collection, this series is designed to make learning fun and rewarding. Connection Phonics books are based on the premise that mastering language skills builds confidence and enhances a student's entire educational experience. A fundamental factor in learning to read is a strong phonics foundation, beginning with an awareness of the alphabet, understanding phonemic relationships and the concept of words, and moving onto word recognition. This workbook is based on core curriculum and is designed to reinforce classroom phonics skills and strategies. Pages include graphics, examples, and simple directions to introduce phonics concepts such as letter and sound recognition, word families, long and short vowels, blends, sight words, beginning and ending sounds, contractions, plurals, prefixes and suffixes, antonyms and synonyms, homophones, and silent letters. Phonics Connection books also provide writing practice.

Dear Parents and Educators,

Thank you for choosing this Rainbow Bridge Publishing educational product to help teach your children and students. We take great pride and pleasure in becoming involved with your educational experience. Some people say that math will always be math and reading will always be reading, but we do not share that opinion. Reading, math, spelling, writing, geography, science, history, and all other subjects will always be some of life's most fulfilling adventures and should be taught with passion both at home and in the classroom. Because of this, we at Rainbow Bridge Publishing associate the greatness of learning with every product we create.

It is our mission to provide materials that not only explain, but also amaze; not only review, but also encourage; not only guide, but also lead. Every product contains clear, concise instructions, appropriate sample work, and engaging, grade-appropriate content created by classroom teachers and writers that is based on national standards to support your best educational efforts. We hope you enjoy our company's products as you embark on your adventure. Thank you for bringing us along.

Sincerely,

George Starks
Rainbow Bridge Publishing

Phonics Connection • Grade 2
Written by Clareen Arnold

Series Creator
Michele Van Leeuwen

Illustrations
Amanda Sorensen

Visual Design and Layout
Andy Carlson, Robyn Funk

Editorial Director
Paul Rawlins

Copy Editors and Proofreaders
Elaine Clark, Kristina Kugler, Lauren Mauery

Special Thanks
Dante J. Orazzi

Please visit our website at
www.summerbridgeactivities.com
for supplements, additions, and corrections to this book.

First Edition 2003

ISBN: 978-1-93221-024-8

PRINTED IN THE UNITED STATES OF AMERICA
10 9 8 7 6 5 4 3 2

Phonics - Grade 2
Table of Contents

Sound and Letters Chart

r(a)t   (a)p(e)   sn(a)il   j(ar)

(au)to   s(aw)   cr(ay)fish   (b)ear

(c)at   (c)entipede   (ch)eetah   (d)eer

(e)lephant   s(ea)l   br(ea)d   b(ee)

f(er)n   n(ew)s   (f)ish   (g)orilla

(g)iraffe   (h)orse   (i)nchworm   crocod(i)l(e)

b(ir)d   (j)aguar   (k)angaroo   (kn)ot

(l)ion   (m)ouse   (n)ewt   go(ng)

    www.summerbridgeactivities.com   **Phonics Connection—Grade 2—RBP0245**

Sound and Letters Chart

Octopus

goat

stone

coin

goose

crow

wood

horn

cloud

cow

boys

pig

quail

rabbit

sun

shark

turtle

thin

thrust

duck

duke

vulture

vase

wolf

whale

write

fox

yak

fly

pony

zebra

www.summerbridgeactivities.com
© RBP Books

Short *i* Word Chunks

Read the words. Say each picture name. Listen for the short *i* sound \ĭ\.
Write the word from the word list. Color the picture.

d(ig)

~~pin~~   ~~fix~~   ~~lid~~   ~~lips~~   ~~kit~~   ~~rib~~   ~~fin~~   ~~pit~~

pin	fin	pit	lips
lid	kit	rib	fix

Read each sentence. Read the words in the word bank. Fill in the circle for the word that completes the sentence. Write that word in the sentence. Draw a picture of the sentence you just made.

The pig liked to __dig__ in the mud.

- ○ hit
- ○ win
- ● dig
- ○ did

Is your fish __big__ or little?

- ● big
- ○ sit
- ○ tin
- ○ rid

The lid did not fit the __dish__.

- ○ it
- ○ fix
- ○ hid
- ● dish

www.summerbridgeactivities.com   Phonics Connection—Grade 2—RBP0245

Short *i* Word Chunks

Read the story below. Say each word. Listen carefully for the short *i*
sound \ĭ\. Draw a line under each word with the short *i* sound.
Write your favorites in the short *i* word bank. Add to or color the picture.

mitt

Once there was a big pink pig
who wore a yellow wig.
He liked to dance an Irish jig.
He danced under the fig tree.
Six purple inchworms hid by a twig
Their eyes fixed on the pig.
The pig tripped on a stick.
The inchworms picked up the pig.
They fixed his hurt lip.

Read each question about the story. Fill in the circle by the correct answer.
Write the word on the line.

1. The pig was _____ .
   o fat   o big   o little   o thin

2. What kind of tree was in the story? _____ .
   o apple   o pear   o fig   o date

Write an answer.

How many inchworms were there?

_____

On another piece of paper write a story about a pig. What can the pig do?
What color is it? How big is it?

Short *i*
Word Bank

big

Short *u* Word Chunks

Read the words. Say the picture names. Draw a line from each word to the picture it names. Circle the short *u* word chunks. Color the pictures.

c(up)

www.summerbridgeactivities.com   Phonics Connection—Grade 2—RBP0245

Short *u* Word Chunks

Read the words. Say each picture name. Listen for the short *u* sound \ŭ\.
Write the word from the word list. Color the picture.

t(u g)

run   sun   nut   jug   hum   rub   tub   cub

run

Read each sentence. Read the words in the word bank. Fill in the circle for the word that completes the sentence. Write that word in the sentence. Draw a picture of the sentence you just made.

Gus put the pup into the _____.	○ tub ○ fun ○ jug ○ gum
The cub is on the _____.	○ rug ○ hum ○ dug ○ nut
A big bug sat in the _____.	○ plug ○ sun ○ much ○ run

Short *u* Word Chunks

Read the story below. Say each word. Listen carefully for the short *u* sound \ŭ\. Draw a line under each word with the short *u* sound. Write your favorites in the short *u* word bank. Add to or color the picture.

bug

Gus was a fun hum bug.

He lived in a hut made of nuts.

He had to find a new home.

He moved to a tub inside a jug.

He took his rug and his cup.

At his new home he could run in the sun.

He could play in the mud.

Read each question about the story. Fill in the circle by the correct answer. Write the word on the line.

1. Gus had to find a new _____.

○ bus   ○ cub   ○ home   ○ tug

2. Gus likes to play in the _____.

○ cut   ○ sun   ○ tug   ○ gum

Write an answer.

What did Gus take to his new home?

_____

_____

On another piece of paper write a story about moving to a new home. What would you take? Where would you go? Whom would you miss?

**Short *u*
Word Bank**

Gus

_____

_____

_____

_____

_____

_____

_____

_____

Short *o* Word Chunks

Read the words. Say the picture names. Draw a line from each word to the picture it names. Circle the short *o* word chunks. Color the pictures.

dog

Phonics Connection—Grade 2—RBP0245   www.summerbridgeactivities.com   ©RBP Books

Name

Short *o* Word Chunks

Read the words. Say each picture name. Listen for the short *o* sound \ŏ\.
Write the word from the word list. Color the picture.

b(ox)

box   fog   cob   rod   jog   pod   hog   pot

box

Read each sentence. Read the words in the word bank. Fill in the circle for the word that completes the sentence. Write that word in the sentence. Draw a picture of the sentence you just made.

My dog likes to sit on the _____ .	○ cot ○ log ○ box ○ pod
The _____ got hot in the sun.	○ mop ○ frog ○ top ○ cob
Mom had to mop up the spill from the _____ .	○ pot ○ dog ○ hog ○ lot

©RBP Books   www.summerbridgeactivities.com   Phonics Connection—Grade 2—RBP0245

Short *o* Word Chunks

Read the story below. Say each word. Listen carefully for the short *o* sound \ŏ\. Draw a line under each word with the short *o* sound. Write your favorites in the short *o* word bank. Add to or color the picture.

dot

One <u>hot</u> foggy day a frog popped out of his pond.

He wanted to find someone to play with him.

He found his friends, Ox and Octopus.

Octopus could mop floors with his eight legs.

Ox could put the pot on the top cot.

Frog could hop from log to log.

They all had to obey Mom when she said, "Stop."

Read each question about the story. Fill in the circle by the correct answer. Write the word on the line.

1. What kind of day was it? _____

    o hot   o cold   o foggy   o warm

2. Who popped out of his pond? _____

    o Frog   o Dog   o Ox   o Octopus

Write an answer.

What could Ox do?

_____

_____

On another piece of paper write about what you and your friends do at your house or their houses.

Short *o* Word Bank

hot

Name

Short *e* Word Chunks

Read the words. Say the picture names. Draw a line from each word to the picture it names. Circle the short *e* word chunks. Color the pictures.

w(et)

w(eb)

w(et)

shell

smell

leg

beg

jet

pet

step

sled

hen

men

bell

well

nest

net

www.summerbridgeactivities.com

Name

Short e Word Chunks

Read the words. Say each picture name. Listen for the short *e* sound \ĕ\.
Write the word from the word list. Color the picture.

jet　　　net　　　ten　　　hen　　　bed　　　leg　　　bell　　　sled

jet

Read each sentence. Read the words in the word bank. Fill in the circle for the word that completes the sentence. Write that word in the sentence. Draw a picture of the sentence you just made.

There were ten spiders in the _____.	◌ bed ◌ web ◌ pen ◌ nest
Jed has a _____ elephant.	◌ leg ◌ pet ◌ men ◌ best
The red hen sat on an _____.	◌ bed ◌ wet ◌ men ◌ egg

Phonics Connection—Grade 2—RBP0245　　　　　www.summerbridgeactivities.com　　　　©RBP Books

Short *e* Word Chunks

Read the story below. Say each word. Listen carefully for the short *e* sound \ĕ\. Draw a line under each word with the short *e* sound. Write your favorites in the word bank. Add to or color the picture.

jet

Have you seen an <u>elephant</u>?
One lives in a big tent.
He has bells on his neck.
He has a huge jet for a hat.
His face is painted red.
Ten men put him in a pen.
The pen had no bed.
The elephant was mad.
He ran away from the circus.
Have you see an elephant?

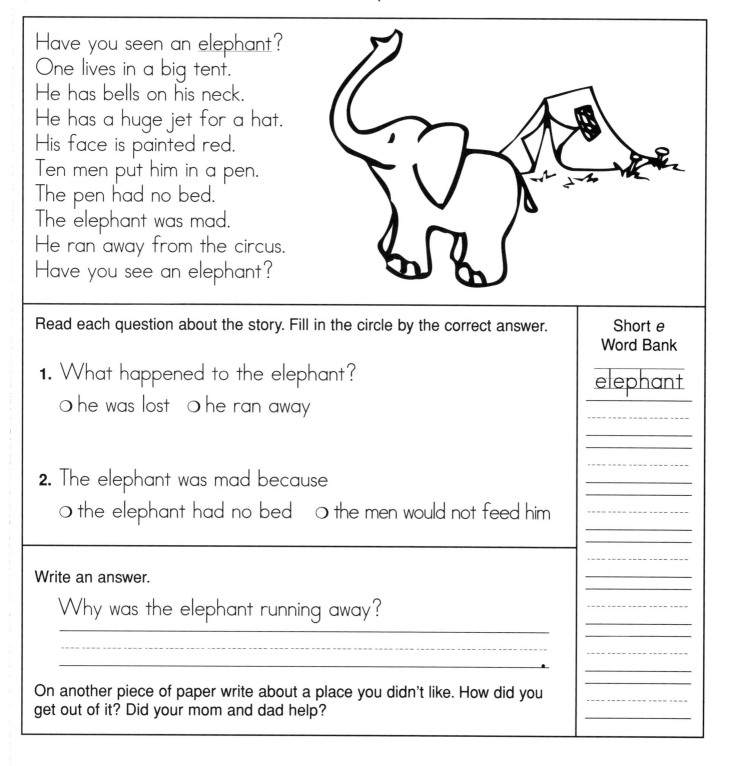

Read each question about the story. Fill in the circle by the correct answer.

1. What happened to the elephant?

○ he was lost   ○ he ran away

2. The elephant was mad because

○ the elephant had no bed   ○ the men would not feed him

Write an answer.

Why was the elephant running away?

_____

_____

On another piece of paper write about a place you didn't like. How did you get out of it? Did your mom and dad help?

Short *e*
Word Bank

elephant
_____
_____
_____
_____
_____
_____
_____
_____
_____
_____
_____

www.summerbridgeactivities.com   Phonics Connection—Grade 2—RBP0245

Long Vowel a (ā)

Read the words. Say the picture names. Draw a line from each word to the picture it names. Write the vowel sounds like the example below. Color the pictures.

lake

Example:

căn   [can]   **cāne̸**   [cane]

Cane has the long *a* sound. This sound is often spelled by ā and silent e̸.

---

căn / cāne̸	cap / cape
man / mane	pan / pane
bat / bake	van / vase
pan / plane	sat / skate

   www.summerbridgeactivities.com   © RBP Books

Long Vowel *a* (ā)

Read the words. Say each picture name. Listen for the long *a* sound \ā\.
Write the word from the word list. Color the picture.

cane

cave   race   tape   safe   cake   cane   rake   snake

cave

_____

_____

_____

_____

_____

_____

_____

Read each sentence. Read the words in the word bank. Fill in the circle for the word that completes the sentence. Write that word in the sentence. Draw a picture of the sentence you just made.

Kate will sail on the _____ .	○ case ○ tape ○ lake ○ late
Dale had to fix a _____ .	○ gate ○ name ○ cape ○ cane
Jake had to play a _____ .	○ same ○ game ○ safe ○ plate

Long Vowel *a* (ā)

Look at each picture below. Fill in the missing letters in the word below the picture. Listen carefully for the long *a* vowel sound \ā\.

plane

Example:

căn   cānẹ

Cane has the long *a* sound. This sound is often spelled by *a* and silent *e*.

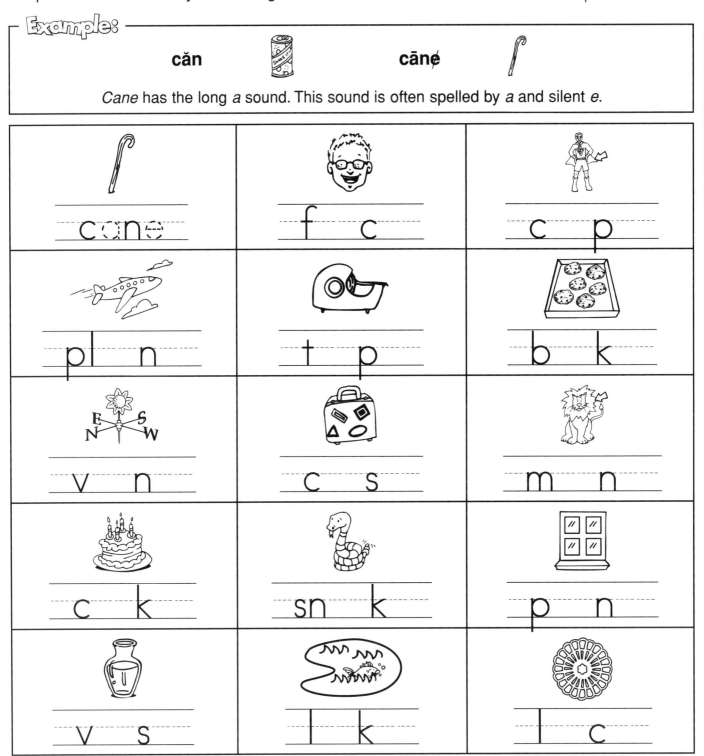

c a n e

f _ c

c _ p

p l _ n

t _ p

b _ k

v _ n

c _ s

m _ n

c _ k

sn _ k

p _ n

v _ s

l _ k

l _ c

Long Vowel *a* (ā)

Read the story below. Say each word. Listen carefully for the long *a* sound \ā\. Draw a line under each word with the long *a* sound. Write your favorites in the long *a* word bank. Add to or color the picture.

rake

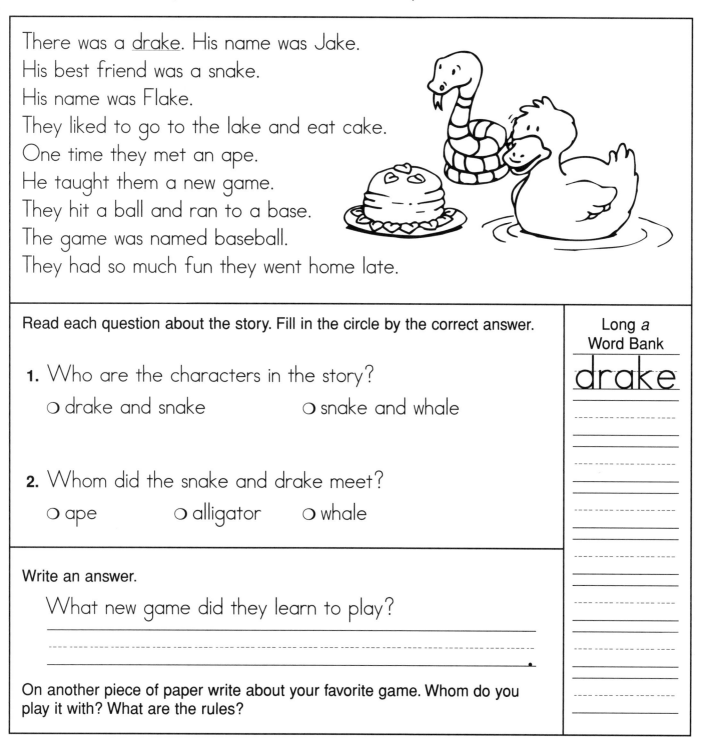

There was a <u>drake</u>. His name was Jake.
His best friend was a snake.
His name was Flake.
They liked to go to the lake and eat cake.
One time they met an ape.
He taught them a new game.
They hit a ball and ran to a base.
The game was named baseball.
They had so much fun they went home late.

Read each question about the story. Fill in the circle by the correct answer.

1. Who are the characters in the story?

○ drake and snake   ○ snake and whale

2. Whom did the snake and drake meet?

○ ape   ○ alligator   ○ whale

Write an answer.

What new game did they learn to play?

_____

On another piece of paper write about your favorite game. Whom do you play it with? What are the rules?

Long *a* Word Bank

drake
_____
_____
_____
_____
_____
_____
_____
_____
_____

www.summerbridgeactivities.com   Phonics Connection—Grade 2—RBP0245

Vowel Digraphs: *ai, ay*

Read the words. Say the picture names. Draw a line from each word to the picture it names. Circle the vowel pair *ai,* or *ay.* Color the pictures.

bait

Example:

rain $\bar{a}i = \bar{a}$ hay $\bar{a}y = \bar{a}$

Two vowels together often stand for the sound of the first vowel.
Rain has a long *a* sound \ā\ spelled *ai. Hay* has a long *a* sound spelled *ay.*

www.summerbridgeactivities.com   ©RBP Books

Vowel Digraphs: *ai, ay*

Read the words. Say each picture name. Listen for the vowel pair *ai* and *ay* sound. Write the word from the word list. Color the picture.

brain

| brain | clay | bait | train | rain | drain | grain | tray |

brain

Read each sentence. Read the words in the word bank. Fill in the circle for the word that completes the sentence. Write that word in the sentence. Draw a picture of the sentence you just made.

Jane put _____ on her hook to catch a fish.	○ bait ○ train ○ rain ○ drain
In art class we build with _____.	○ clay ○ tray ○ ray ○ may
I got a pizza _____ on my dress.	○ stain ○ chain ○ drain ○ rain

www.summerbridgeactivities.com

Phonics Connection—Grade 2—RBP0245

Name

Vowel Digraphs: *ai, ay*

Look at each picture below. Fill in the missing letters in the word below the picture. Listen carefully for the vowel pairs *ai* and *ay*.

rain

Example:

rain āi = ā 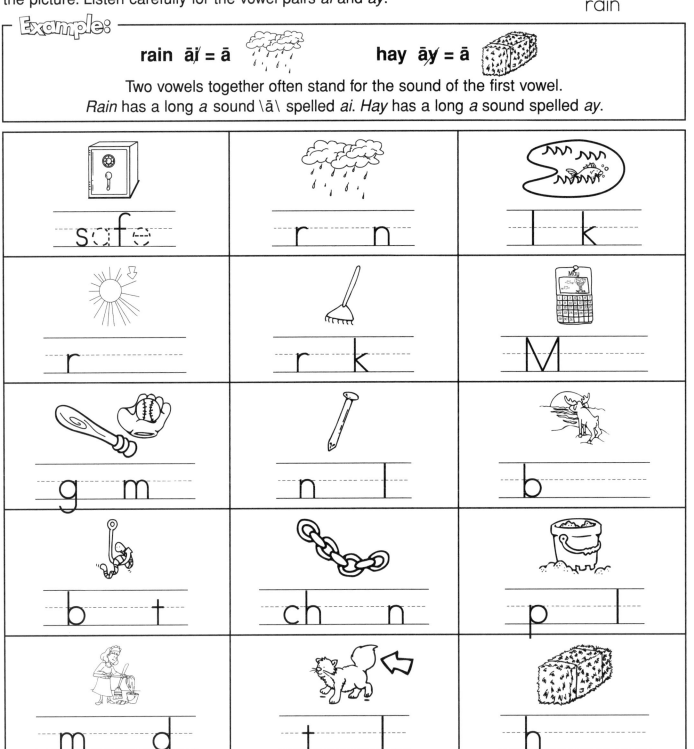   hay āy = ā

Two vowels together often stand for the sound of the first vowel.
Rain has a long *a* sound \ā\ spelled *ai*. *Hay* has a long *a* sound spelled *ay*.

s a f e	r __ __ n	l __ k
r __ __	r __ k	M __ __
g __ m	n __ l	b __ __
b __ t	ch __ n	p __ l
m __ d	t __ l	h __

Phonics Connection—Grade 2—RBP0245   www.summerbridgeactivities.com   ©RBP Books

Vowel Digraphs: *ai, ay*

Read the story below. Listen carefully for the vowel pairs *ai* and *ay*
Draw a line under each word with the vowel pair *ai* or *ay*. Write your
favorites in the vowel digraph word bank. Add to or color the picture.

ray

A <u>maid</u> named Lorraine lived in Maine.
She went on a train to the beach in May.
She took her dog. He was a Great Dane.
She wanted to fish in the lake.
She put bait on her hook.
Sitting and waiting was a strain.
Then it started to rain.
It was a hurricane!
She got back on the train.
She went home to Maine.

Read each question about the story. Fill in the circle by the correct answer.
Write the word on the line.

1. Lorraine was a _____

○ brain   ○ maid   ○ ray   ○ chain

2. A Great Dane is a _____

○ cat   ○ dog   ○ pig   ○ fish

Write an answer.

List the kinds of bait she might use on her hook to catch a fish.

_____

On another piece of paper write a story about a time you went fishing. Did
you catch a fish? What bait did you use? How big was the fish?

Vowel Digraph
Word Bank

maid

Long Vowel *i* (ī)

Read the words. Say the picture names. Draw a line from each word to the picture it names. Mark the long *i* words like the example below. Color the pictures.

hike

Example:

pĭn **pīnè** (pine tree image)

When a word has two vowels, and one is final *e*, the first vowel is long and the *e* is silent.

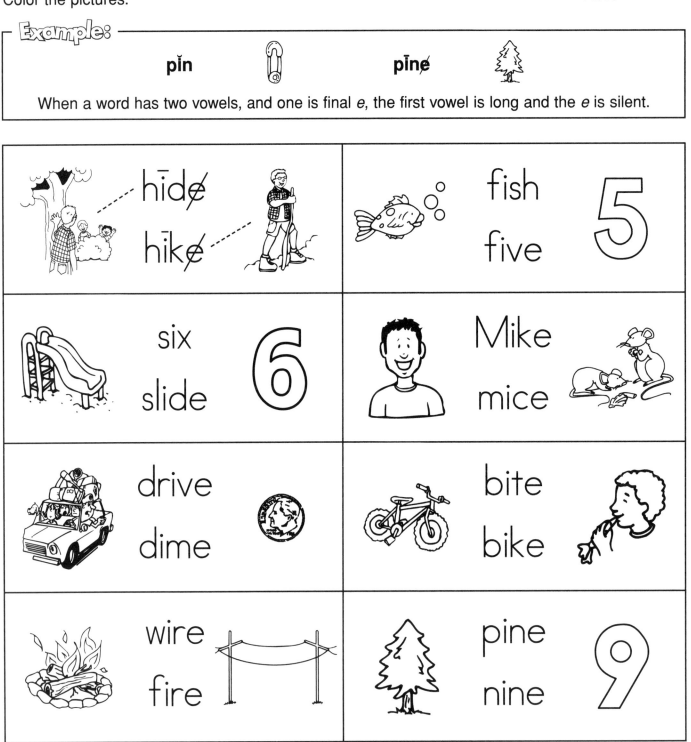

hīdè
hīkè

fish
five 5

six
slide 6

Mike
mice

drive
dime

bite
bike

wire
fire

pine
nine 9

Name

Long Vowel *i* (ī)

Read the words. Say each picture name. Listen for the long *i* vowel sound \ī\. Write the word from the word list. Color the picture.

vine

dive   vine   ride   bride   spider   smile   climb   pipe

dive

Read each sentence. Read the words in the word bank. Fill in the circle for the word that completes the sentence. Write that word in the sentence. Draw a picture of the sentence you just made.

Sam put a _____ on his car.	○ file ○ tire ○ dice ○ fire
We painted our house _____.	○ wife ○ white ○ wit ○ wide
I like to sit under the _____ trees.	○ pin ○ pipe ○ pine ○ pie

www.summerbridgeactivities.com   Phonics Connection—Grade 2—RBP0245

Name

Long Vowel *i* (ī)

Look at each picture below. Fill in the missing letters in the word below the picture. Listen carefully for the long *i* vowel sound \ī\.

pine

Example:

pĭn   pīne

When a word has two vowels, and one is final *e*, the first vowel is long and the *e* is silent.

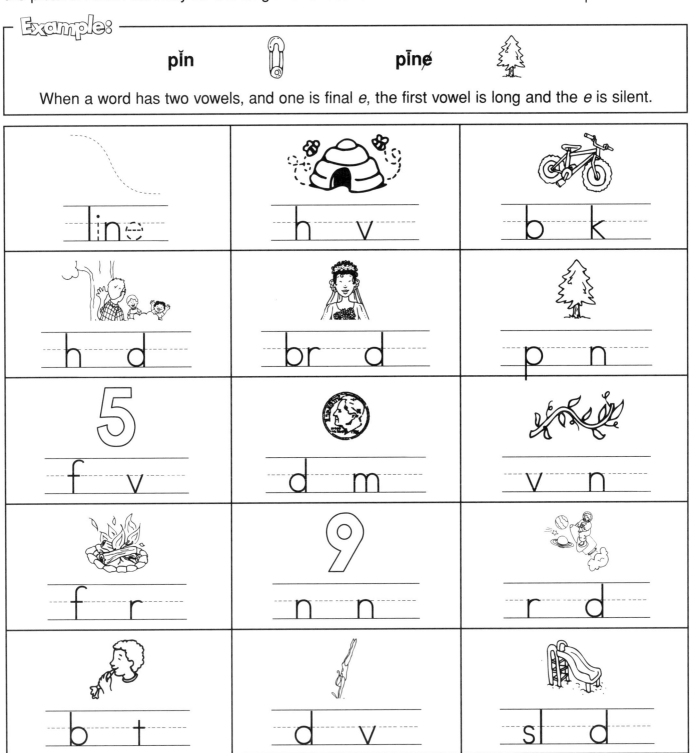

l i n e	h __ v __	b __ k __
h __ d __	br __ d __	p __ n __
f __ v __	d __ m __	v __ n __
f __ r __	n __ n __	r __ d __
b __ t __	d __ v __	s l __ d __

Phonics Connection—Grade 2—RBP0245   www.summerbridgeactivities.com   ©RBP Books

Long Vowel *i* (*ī*)

Read the story below. Say each word. Listen carefully for the long *i* vowel sound \ī\. Draw a line under each word with the long *i* vowel sound. Write your favorites in the long *i* word bank. Add to or color the picture.

kite

My name is <u>Mike</u>.
Each day I ride my white bike.
I fly my kite.
I eat lime pie.
I climb the pine trees.
I go down the slide.
I catch five fish.
I spend nine dimes.
I play with my nice mice.
I climb into bed at night.
I have a fine life.

Read each question about the story. Fill in the circle by the correct answer. Write the word on the line.

Long *i* Word Bank

Mike

1. Mike had a _____ life.

    ○ fine   ○ five   ○ nine   ○ line

2. He likes to ride his _____ bike.

    ○ white   ○ kite   ○ slide   ○ wide

Write an answer.

What kind of trees did Mike like to climb?

_____

_____

On another piece of paper make a list of what you do each day.

Long Vowel *u* (ū)

Read the words. Say the picture names. Draw a line from each word to the picture it names. Mark the sounds of the words like the example below. Color the picture.

cute

Example:

When a word had two vowels, and one is final *e*, the first vowel is long and the *e* is silent.

cūbé

When two vowels are together, the first vowel is usually long and the second is silent.

glūé

cub
cūbé

tub
tube

fudge
flute

June
glue

cut
cute

mud
mule

rug
rule

cup
cubes

www.summerbridgeactivities.com © RBP Books

Long Vowel *u* (ū)

Read the words. Say each picture name. Listen for the long *u* vowel sound \ū\.
Write the word from the word list. Color the picture.

mule

glue   fuse   bugle   chute   juice   tune   fuel   fruit

glue

Read each sentence. Read the words in the word bank. Fill in the circle for the word that completes the sentence. Write that word in the sentence. Draw a picture of the sentence you just made.

Luke can use the _____ to fix his picture.	○ glue ○ flag ○ frog ○ fat
Ruth had a _____ kitten.	○ cute ○ cut ○ cub ○ cup
Sue can hum a _____.	○ tune ○ tub ○ June ○ tot

     www.summerbridgeactivities.com   Phonics Connection—Grade 2—RBP0245

Name

Long Vowel *u* (ū)

Look at each picture below. Fill in the missing letters in the word below
the picture. Listen carefully for the long *u* sound \ū\.

cube

┌─ Example: ───┐

When a word had two vowels, and one is final *e*, the first vowel is long and the *e* is silent.

cūbe̸

When two vowels are together, the first vowel is usually long and the second is silent.

glūe̸

└──┘

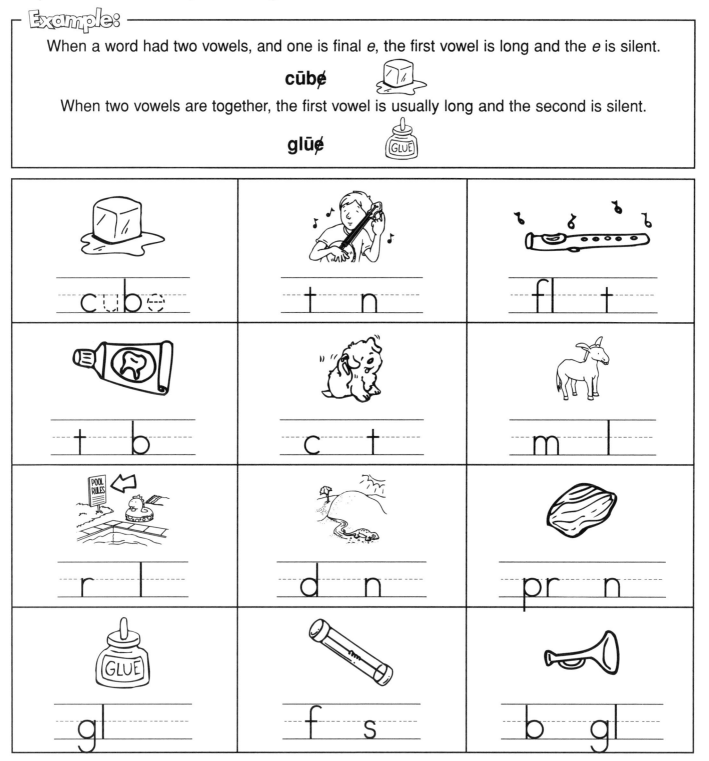

c u b e	t __ n	fl __ t
t __ b __	c __ t	m __ l __
r __ l __	d __ n	pr __ n
gl __ __	f __ s __	b __ gl __

Phonics Connection—Grade 2—RBP0245   www.summerbridgeactivities.com   © RBP Books

Long Vowel *u* (ū)

glue

Read the story below. Say each word. Listen carefully for the long *u* vowel sound \ū\. Draw a line under each word with the long *u* vowel sound. Write your favorites in the long *u* word bank. Add to or color the picture.

Sue was a spy.
She was due to find a clue.
She rode her mule to the dunes.
She took water with her.
That was the rule.
She played a tune on the flute as she rode on the mule.
In the dunes she found a tube of blue paint.
The paint tube had fingerprints on it.
That was the clue she needed.

Read each question about the story. Fill in the circle by the correct answer. Write the word on the line.

1. Sue was a _____.

   O spy   O pie   O camel   O pup

2. She rode a _____.

   O bike   O mule   O horse   O camel

Write an answer.

What was the clue Sue was looking for?

_____

_____

On another piece of paper write the story again. This time, help Sue find a different clue.

Long *u*
Word Bank

Sue
_____
_____
_____
_____
_____
_____
_____
_____

© RBP Books   www.summerbridgeactivities.com   Phonics Connection—Grade 2—RBP0245

Long Vowel *o* (ō)

Read the words. Say the picture names. Draw a line from each word to the picture it names. Mark the vowel sounds like the example below. Color the picture.

nose

Example:

When a word has two vowels, and one is final *e*, the first vowel is long and the *e* is silent.

rōsé

When two vowels are together, the first vowel is usually long and the second is silent.

tōad   **tōé**

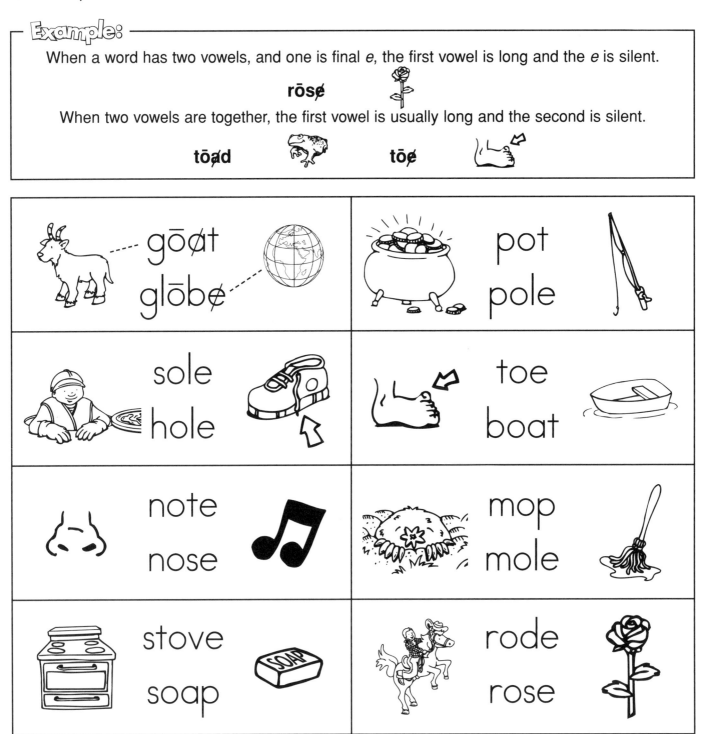

gōat
glōbé

pot
pole

sole
hole

toe
boat

note
nose

mop
mole

stove
soap

rode
rose

Phonics Connection—Grade 2—RBP0245   www.summerbridgeactivities.com   ©RBP Books

Long Vowel *o* (ō)

Read the words. Say each picture name. Listen for the long *o* vowel sound \ō\.
Write the word from the word list. Color the picture.

rose

toe   stone   hoe   nose   coat   robe   soap   wrote

toe

Read each sentence. Read the words in the word bank. Fill in the circle for the word that completes the sentence. Write that word in the sentence. Draw a picture of the sentence you just made.

A toad is in the _____.	○ rod ○ road ○ rag ○ robe
A mole is in the _____.	○ hat ○ hole ○ hot ○ hoe
You can smell the rose with your _____.	○ not ○ nose ○ note ○ hose

Long Vowel *o* (ō)

toad

Look at each picture below. Fill in the missing letters in the word below the picture. Listen carefully for the long *o* vowel sound \ō\.

Example:

When a word has two vowels, and one is final *e*, the first vowel is long and the *e* is silent.

rōsℓ

When two vowels are together, the first vowel is usually long and the second is silent.

tōₐd   **tōℓ**

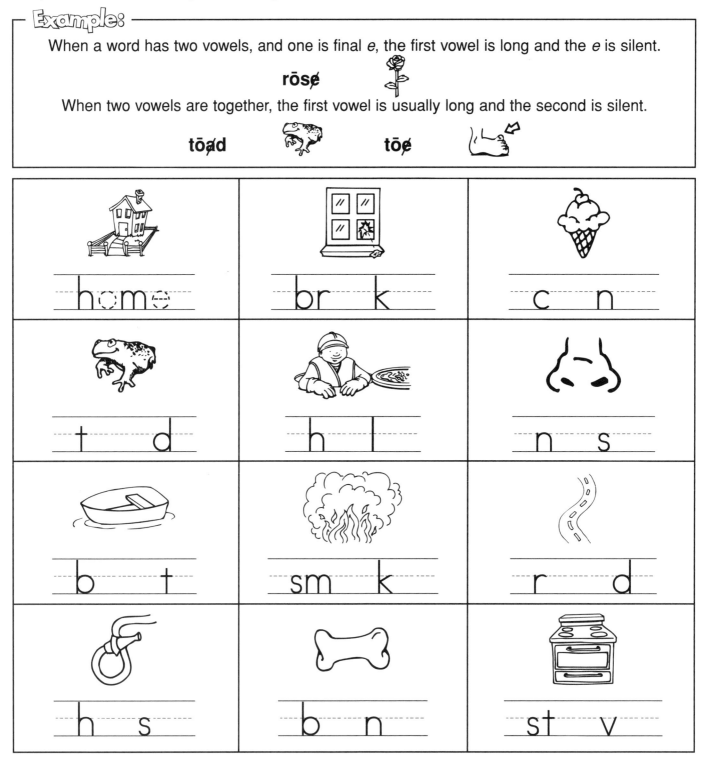

h o m e	br _ k	c _ n
t _ d	h _ l	n _ s
b _ t	sm _ k	r _ d
h _ s	b _ n	st _ v

Long Vowel o (ō)

Read the story below. Say each word. Listen carefully for the long o vowel sound \ō\. Draw a line under each word with the long o vowel sound. Write your favorites in the long o word bank. Add to or color the picture.

toe

Joan and her goat went for a ride.
They went for a ride in a boat.
They floated on the moat.
A toad jumped into the boat.
He wanted to tell them a joke.
The toad's joke was funny.
Joan broke out laughing,
but the goat groaned.
As quickly as the toad hopped
in, he hopped out again.

Knock, Knock...

Read each question about the story. Fill in the circle by the correct answer. Write the word on the line.

1. Joan went in a boat with a _____.

   ○ coat   ○ goat   ○ gold   ○ goal

2. The toad told a _____.

   ○ story   ○ joke   ○ poem   ○ song

Write an answer.

How would you feel if someone hopped in your boat?

_____

_____

On another piece of paper write the funniest joke you have ever heard.

Long o Word Bank

Joan

_____

_____

_____

_____

_____

_____

_____

_____

_____

_____

_____

Name

Long Vowel e (ē)

Read the words. Say the picture names. Draw a line from each word to
the picture it names. Mark the vowel sounds like the example below. Color
the picture.

bee

Example:

jēep 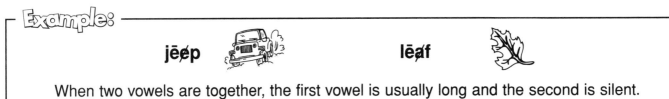   lēaf

When two vowels are together, the first vowel is usually long and the second is silent.

pēa

sēa

beach

peach

bead

beak

heel

wheel

seed

jeep

feet

flea

three

tree

beet

bean

Phonics Connection—Grade 2—RBP0245   www.summerbridgeactivities.com

Long Vowel e (ē)

Read the words. Say each picture name. Listen for the long *e* vowel sound \ē\. Write the word from the word list. Color the picture.

pea

seal   seat   leaf   heat   sheep   bee   peek   knee

seal   _____   _____   _____

_____   _____   _____   _____

Read each sentence. Read the words in the word bank. Fill in the circle for the word that completes the sentence. Write that word in the sentence. Draw a picture of the sentence you just made.

Do you like roast _____ ?	○ beef ○ wheat ○ peach ○ leaf
The farmer had nine _____ .	○ ships ○ sheep ○ seat ○ shape
The children were eating _____ .	○ heat ○ knees ○ meatballs ○ bees

Long Vowel e (ē)

Look at each picture below. Fill in the missing letters in the word below
the picture. Listen carefully for the long *e* vowel sound \ē\.

tree

Example:

jēep 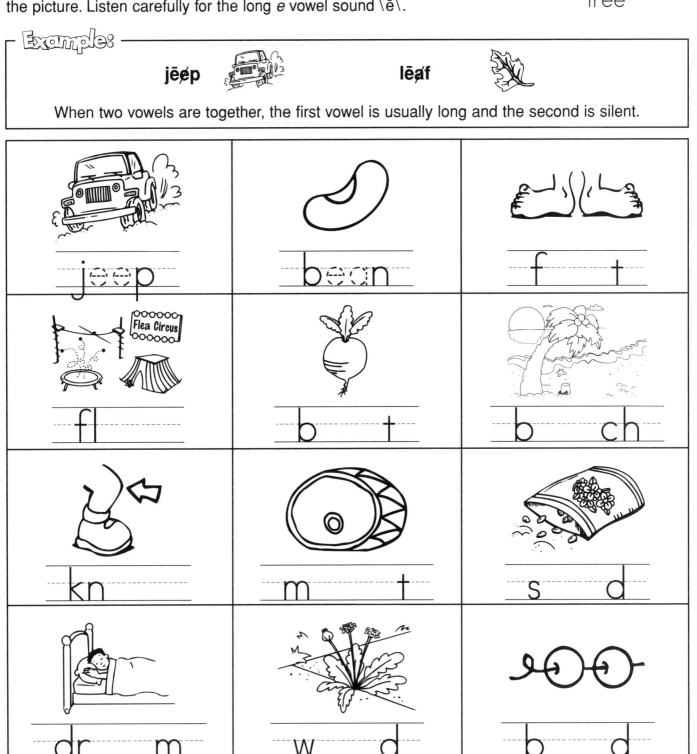   lēaf

When two vowels are together, the first vowel is usually long and the second is silent.

j__ __p   b__ __n   f__ __t

fl__ __   b__ __t   b__ __ch

kn__ __   m__ __t   s__ __d

dr__ __m   w__ __d   b__ __d

Long Vowel e (ē)

Read the story below. Say each word. Listen carefully for the long e vowel sound \ē\. Draw a line under each word with the long e vowel sound. Write your favorites in the long e word bank. Add to or color the picture.

wheel

Flea went to Sheep's house to eat a meal.
Sheep brought Flea some peas.
Flea said, "I do not want peas."
So, Sheep brought him beets.
Flea said, " I do not want beets."
So, Sheep brought him weeds.
"Weeds?" screeched Flea. "I want something sweet."
So, Sheep brought him nothing more.
Sheep sat down to eat peaches and cream.

Read each question about the story. Fill in the circle by the correct answer. Write the word on the line.

Long e Word Bank

flea

1. Do you think Flea was _____?
  ○ nice   ○ tired   ○ mean   ○ angry

2. What did Flea want? _____
  ○ beets   ○ peas   ○ pie   ○ something sweet

Write an answer.

What would you have done if you were the sheep?

_____

_____.

On another piece of paper write about a time you had to eat something you didn't like or want. How did it make you feel?

www.summerbridgeactivities.com   Phonics Connection—Grade 2—RBP0245

Name

Sounds of y

Read the words. Say the picture names. Draw a line from each word to the picture it names. Write in whether the y sounds like *y*, *i*, or *e*. Follow the example. Color the picture.

story

Example:

The letter *y* has a sound of \y\, as in *yak*. The letter *y* at the end of some words can stand for the long *i* sound \ī\ as in *fly*. The letter *y* at the end of some words can also stand for the long *e* sound \ē\ as in *story*.

yak   **fly = flī**   **story = storē**

fly = i
city = e

yam =
pony =

sky =
dreamy =

cry =
penny =

yak =
puppy =

dry =
daddy =

buy =
bunny =

spy =
sleepy =

52

Phonics Connection—Grade 2—RBP0245   www.summerbridgeactivities.com   ©RBP Books

Name

Sounds of y

Read the words. Say each picture name. Listen for the sound of *y*.
Write the word from the word list. Color the picture.

candy

candy   daddy   fly   bunny   cry   muddy   party   fifty

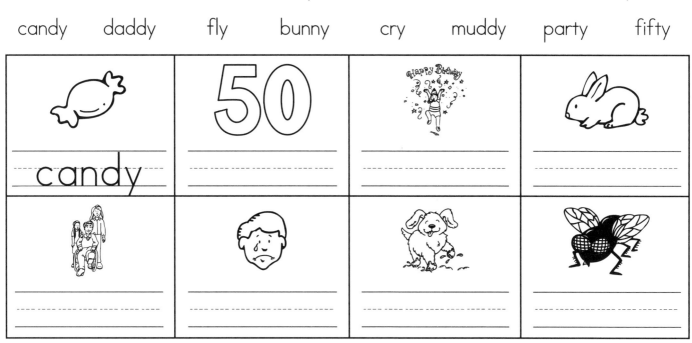

candy _____   _____   _____   _____

_____   _____   _____   _____

Read each sentence. Read the words in the word bank. Fill in the circle for the word that completes the sentence. Write that word in the sentence. Draw a picture of the sentence you just made.

Our boots were _____.	○ fifty ○ muddy ○ bunny ○ fly
We went to the store to get a _____.	○ penny ○ yo-yo ○ party ○ cry
Did you see the eagle in the _____?	○ pie ○ sly ○ sky ○ fry

Name

Sounds of y

Look at each picture below. Fill in the missing letters in the word below the picture. Listen carefully for all the different *y* sounds.

baby

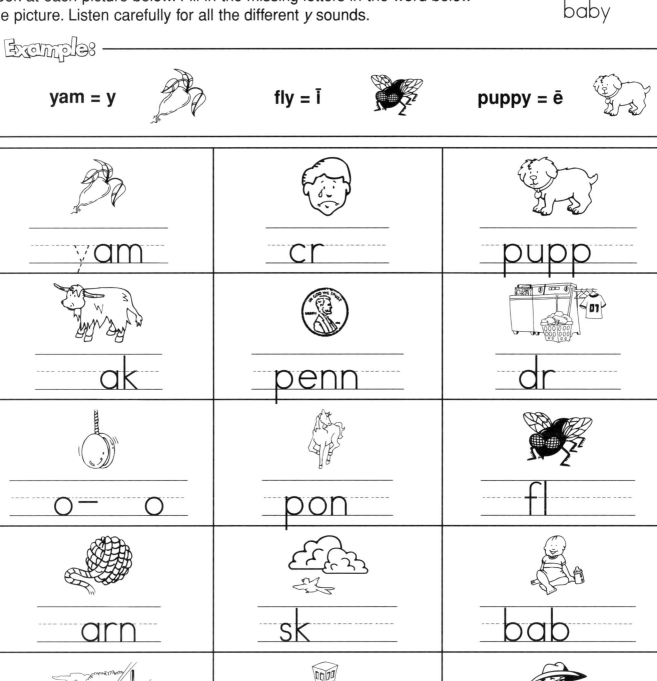

Example:

yam = y   fly = ī   puppy = ē

yam	cr___	pupp___
___ak	penn___	dr___
o-___o	pon___	fl___
___arn	sk___	bab___
___ard	cit___	sp___

Phonics Connection—Grade 2—RBP0245   www.summerbridgeactivities.com   © RBP Books

Sounds of y

Read the story below. Say each word. Listen carefully for the sound of *y*. Draw a line under each word with the sound of *y*. Write your favorites in the *y* word bank. Add to or color the picture.

fly

Ziggy the pink piggy was very shy.
She was having a birthday party.
She invited Benny the white bunny.
She invited Teddy the blue fly.
Benny gave her a yellow daisy.
Teddy gave her sticky green candy.
They all ate a big cream pie.
Benny the white bunny said, "Good-bye."
Then Teddy the blue fly said, "Good-bye."

Read each question about the story. Fill in the circle by the correct answer. Write the word on the line.

1. Ziggy the pink piggy was _____.
    ○ shy   ○ picky   ○ sleepy   ○ lazy

2. Benny the bunny was what color? _____
    ○ green   ○ black   ○ orange   ○ white

Write an answer.

What did Benny the bunny give Ziggy for her birthday?

_____

On another piece of paper write about your favorite birthday party. Now, write about your worst birthday party.

y Word Bank

Ziggy

Name

Hard and Soft c

Read the words. Say the picture names. Draw a line from each word to the picture it names. In the square write the *c* sound for that picture. Color the picture.

Example:

The letter *c* followed by *e*, *i*, or *y* usually stands for the soft *c*, as in *mice*.
The letter *c* followed by any other letter usually stands for the hard sound of *c*, as in *cat*.

mice = s   **cat = k**

☐ k =cub
☐ s =city

☐ =cute
☐ =cent

☐ =rice
☐ =crab

☐ =cave
☐ =cell

☐ =clam
☐ =race

☐ =clay
☐ =mice

☐ =lace
☐ =coat

☐ =cot
☐ =ice

Phonics Connection—Grade 2—RBP0245 www.summerbridgeactivities.com

Name

Hard and Soft *c*

Read the words. Say each picture name. Listen for the hard and soft *c*. Write the word from the word list. Color the picture.

cap   lace   calf   face   fence   cube   circus   cane

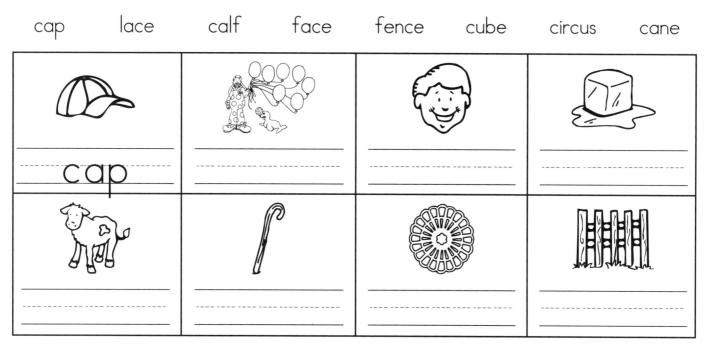

cap

Read each sentence. Fill in the circle for the word that makes the same sound as the underlined word. Draw a picture of the sentence you just made.

The letter *c* followed by *e*, *i*, or *y* usually stands for the soft *c*, as in *mice*. The letter *c* followed by any other letter usually stands for the hard sound of *c*, as in *cat*.

The <u>crab</u> lives on the beach.	○ k ○ s
The <u>mice</u> chased the cat.	○ k ○ s
A camel called home on his <u>cell</u> phone.	○ k ○ s

www.summerbridgeactivities.com   Phonics Connection—Grade 2—RBP0245

Name

Hard and Soft *g*

Read the words. Say the picture names. Draw a line from each word to the picture it names. In the box write the sound of the hard *g* with the letter *g* or soft *g* with the letter *j*. Color the picture.

> **Example:**
> The letter *g* followed by *e*, *i*, or *y* often stands for the soft sound of *g*, as in *giraffe*. The letter *g* followed by any other letter usually stands for the hard sound of *g*, as in *goat*.
>
> **ge, gi, gy = j**   **g)iraffe = j**   **gu, go, ga = g**   **g)oat = g**

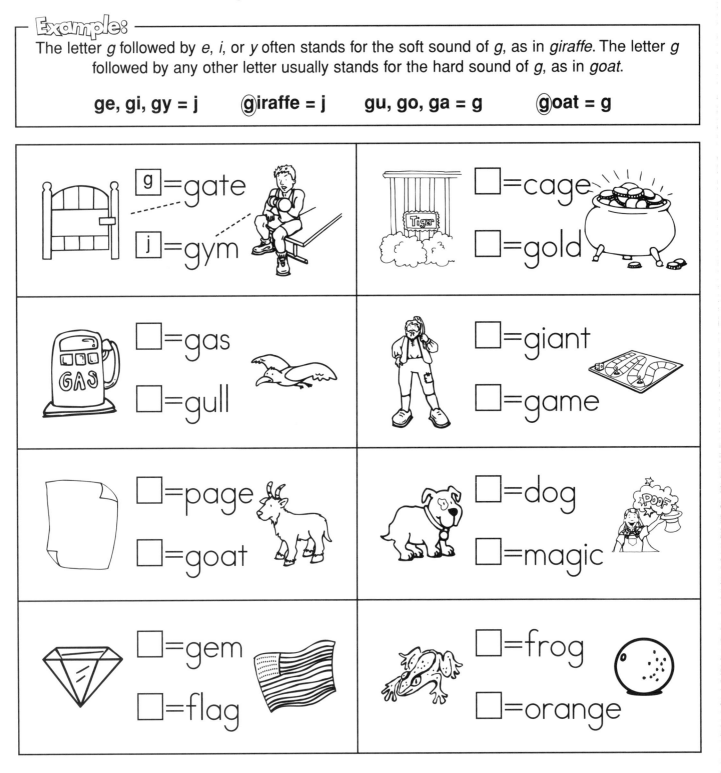

g = gate
j = gym

☐ = cage
☐ = gold

☐ = gas
☐ = gull

☐ = giant
☐ = game

☐ = page
☐ = goat

☐ = dog
☐ = magic

☐ = gem
☐ = flag

☐ = frog
☐ = orange

58

Hard *g* or Soft *g*

Read the words. Say each picture name. Listen for the hard *g* or the soft *g* sound. Write the word from the word list under the picture. Color the picture.

gorilla   pigeon   gas   gift   giraffe   bridge   goat   judge

gorilla

Read each sentence. Fill in the circle for the word that makes the same sound as the underlined word. Draw a picture of the sentence you just made.

The letter *g* followed by *e*, *i*, or *y* often stands for the soft sound of *g*, as in *giraffe*. The letter *g* followed by any other letter usually stands for the hard sound of *g*, as in *goat*.

giraffe = j   **goat = g**

The giant was <u>huge</u>.	○ g ○ j
A green <u>frog</u> ate a black bug.	○ g ○ j
A tall <u>giraffe</u> can't touch his nose to his toes.	○ g ○ j

www.summerbridgeactivities.com   **Phonics Connection—Grade 2—RBP0245**

Hard and Soft *g*

Read the story below. Say each word. Listen carefully for the hard *g* and *c* and the soft *g* and *c* sounds. Draw a line under each word with the hard *g* and hard *c*, or the soft *g* and soft *c*. Write your favorites in the correct word bank. Add to or color the picture.

Brandon's favorite <u>place</u> was the zoo.
He liked how the cages looked like different places.
First, he visited Farm Land.
He laughed as the goat ate the lace on a lady's coat.
Second, he rode a camel.
It was great sitting up so high.
Third, he checked out the red-eyed tree frogs.
Their eyes were bright red and orange.
Last, he went into the cave to see the cute baby bear cubs.
The cub's mother chased him OUT!

Read each question about the story. Fill in the circle by the correct answer. Write the word on the line.

Hard *g* and *c* Word Bank

1. What was Brandon's favorite place? _____
   ○ farm   ○ zoo   ○ garden   ○ race

2. What did the goat eat? _____
   ○ lace   ○ rice   ○ grass   ○ cookies

Soft *c* and *g* Word Bank

place

Write an answer.
   What colors were the eyes of the tree frogs?

_____

On another piece of paper write about your favorite place to visit in the zoo. Share it with one other person.

Phonics Connection—Grade 2—RBP0245   www.summerbridgeactivities.com   ©RBP Books

Initial Consonant Digraphs: *ch, sh, th, wh*

Read the words. Say the picture names. Listen for the first sound. Draw a line from each word to the picture it names. Circle the *ch*, *sh*, *th*, and *wh* consonant pairs. Color the pictures.

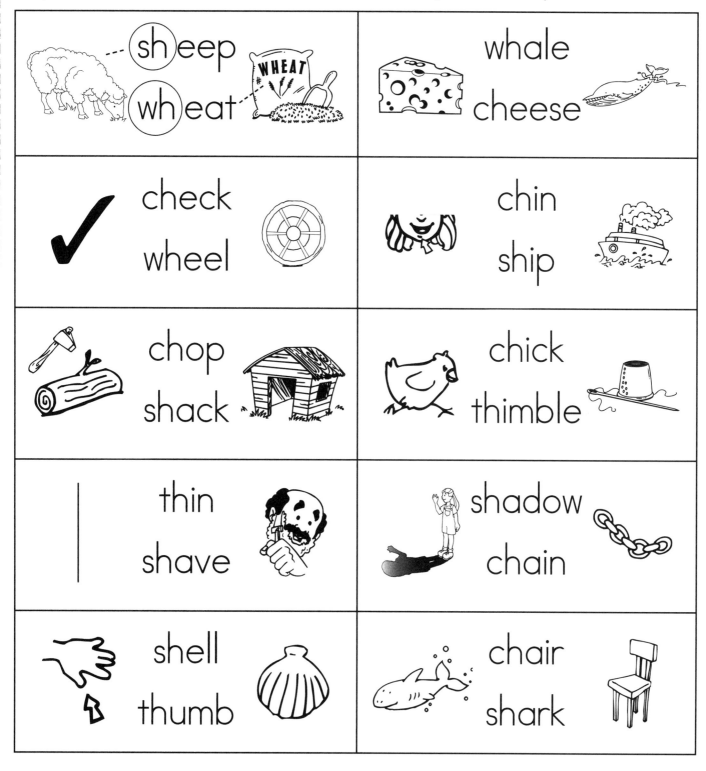

Initial Consonant Digraphs: *ch, sh, th, wh*

Read the words. Say each picture name. Listen for the *ch*, *sh*, *th*, or *wh* sound. Write the word from the word list. Color the picture.

wheel   thumb   shed   child   ship   cheese   thirty   whistle

Read each sentence. Read the words in the word bank. Fill in the circle for the word that completes the sentence. Write that word in the sentence. Draw a picture of the sentence you just made.

We saw a _____ in the ocean.	○ whistle ○ whale ○ wheel ○ white
The teacher wrote on the _____ board.	○ chalk ○ chair ○ cheetah ○ chin
My _____ has a hole in the sole.	○ shoe ○ shave ○ sheep ○ shell

Initial Consonant Digraphs: *ch, sh, th, wh*

Look at each picture below. Fill in the missing letters in the word below the picture. Listen carefully for the *ch, sh, th,* or *wh* sound.

Example:

(ch)eese   (sh)eep   (th)umb   (wh)ale

sh eep   imble   ale

eat   ack   eese

eck   umb   ain

eel   ark   ell

Initial Consonant Digraphs: *ch, sh, th, wh*

Read the story below. Say each word. Listen carefully for the consonant pairs *ch, sh, th,* and *wh*. Draw a line under each word with the consonant pairs *ch, sh, th,* or *wh*. Write your favorites in the word bank. Add to or color the picture.

In the ocean there was a big commotion.
The shark said, "I am the champion."
The whale said, "No, I am the champion."
So, they had a race.
The whistle blew, and a great whoop
went up from all the animals.
Off went the shark and the whale.
They swam down to the shrimp,
around the giant seashell, and
the race ended at the ship.
The judges were the cheetah, chick, and sheep.

I am the champion.

No, I am the champion.

Read each question about the story. Fill in the circle by the correct answer. Write the word on the line.

1. Who was one of the judges? _____

   ○ shark   ○ whale   ○ shrimp   ○ cheetah

2. What sound started the race? _____

   ○ whistle   ○ pistol   ○ thistle   ○ whoop

Write an answer.

Where were the shark and the whale swimming to?

_____

_____.

On another piece of paper write what happens at the end of the race. Who wins the race?

Digraph Word Bank

shark

_____

_____

_____

_____

_____

_____

_____

_____

_____

_____

Phonics Connection—Grade 2—RBP0245   www.summerbridgeactivities.com   ©RBP Books

Name

Final Consonant Digraphs and Trigraphs: *ch, ck, gh, ng, nk, sh, th, tch*

Read the words. Say the picture names. Draw a line from each word to the picture it names. Circle the consonant group: *ch, ck, gh, ng, nk, sh, th, tch*. Color the picture.

bea(ch)

si(ng)

ditch

ink

coach

string

check

sink

peach

ring

deck

trunk

catch

dish

duck

bath

witch

fish

king

math

© RBP Books   www.summerbridgeactivities.com   Phonics Connection—Grade 2—RBP0245

Name

Final Consonant Digraphs and Trigraphs: *ch, ck, gh, ng, nk, sh, th, tch*

Read the words. Say each picture name. Listen for the consonant group: *ch, ck, gh, ng, nk, sh, th, tch.* Write the word from the word list. Color the picture.

pouch   tooth   fetch   patch   back   slick   ring   trash

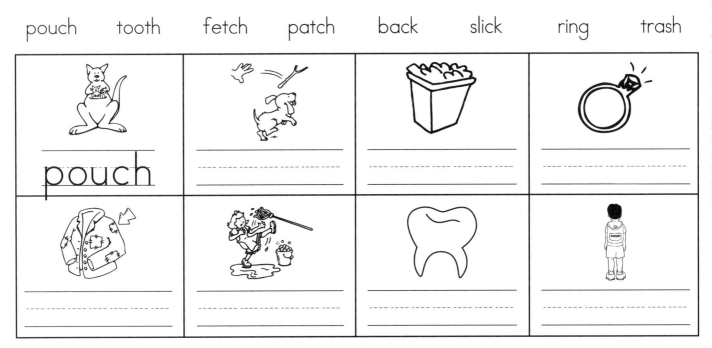

pouch

Read each sentence. Read the words in the word bank. Fill in the circle for the word that completes the sentence. Write that word in the sentence. Draw a picture of the sentence you just made.

Jane likes to sit on the _____ and eat a peach.	○ beach ○ teach ○ itch ○ peach
John let the water down the _____.	○ ditch ○ patch ○ catch ○ witch
Kate has a golden _____ that can sing.	○ check ○ duck ○ deck ○ luck

Phonics Connection—Grade 2—RBP0245   www.summerbridgeactivities.com   ©RBP Books

Name

Final Consonant Digraphs and Trigraphs: *ch, ck, gh, ng, nk, sh, th, tch*

Look at each picture below. Fill in the missing letters in the word below the picture. Listen for the consonant groups: *ch, ck, gh, ng, nk, sh, th, tch*.

bea c h

si ___

coa ___

stri ___

pea ___

ri ___

ba ___

di ___

wi ___

fi ___

di ___

si ___

Final Consonant Digraphs and Trigraphs

Read the story below. Say each word. Listen for the consonant groups: *ch, ck, gh, ng, nk, sh, th, tch.* Draw a line under each word with consonant groups. Write your favorites in the word bank. Add to or color the picture.

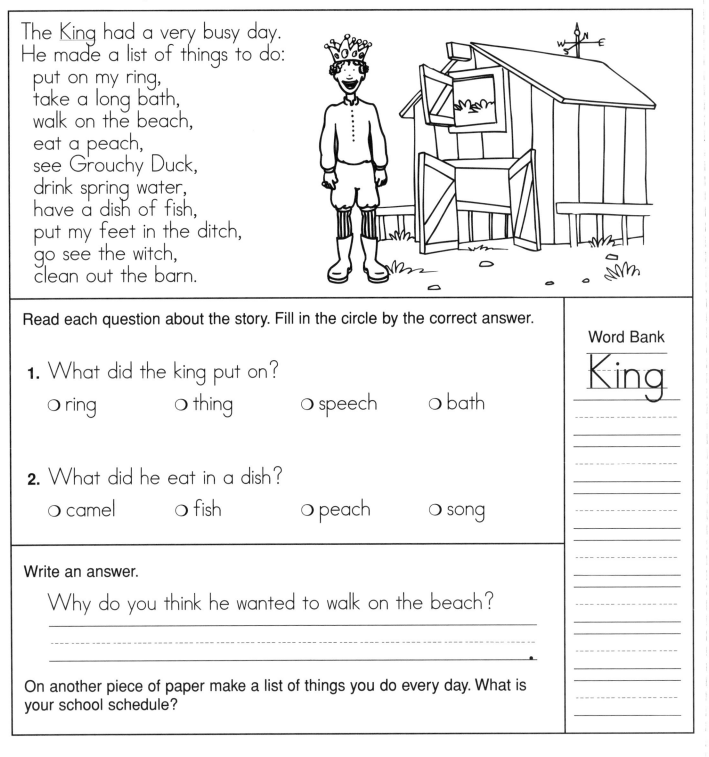

The King had a very busy day.
He made a list of things to do:
  put on my ring,
  take a long bath,
  walk on the beach,
  eat a peach,
  see Grouchy Duck,
  drink spring water,
  have a dish of fish,
  put my feet in the ditch,
  go see the witch,
  clean out the barn.

Read each question about the story. Fill in the circle by the correct answer.

Word Bank

King

1. What did the king put on?

  ○ ring   ○ thing   ○ speech   ○ bath

2. What did he eat in a dish?

  ○ camel   ○ fish   ○ peach   ○ song

Write an answer.

Why do you think he wanted to walk on the beach?

On another piece of paper make a list of things you do every day. What is your school schedule?

Name

Initial *s* Clusters: *sc, sk, sn, sp, st, sm, sw, sq*

Read the words. Say the picture names. Draw a line from each word to the picture it names. Circle the initial *s* cluster in each word. Color the picture.

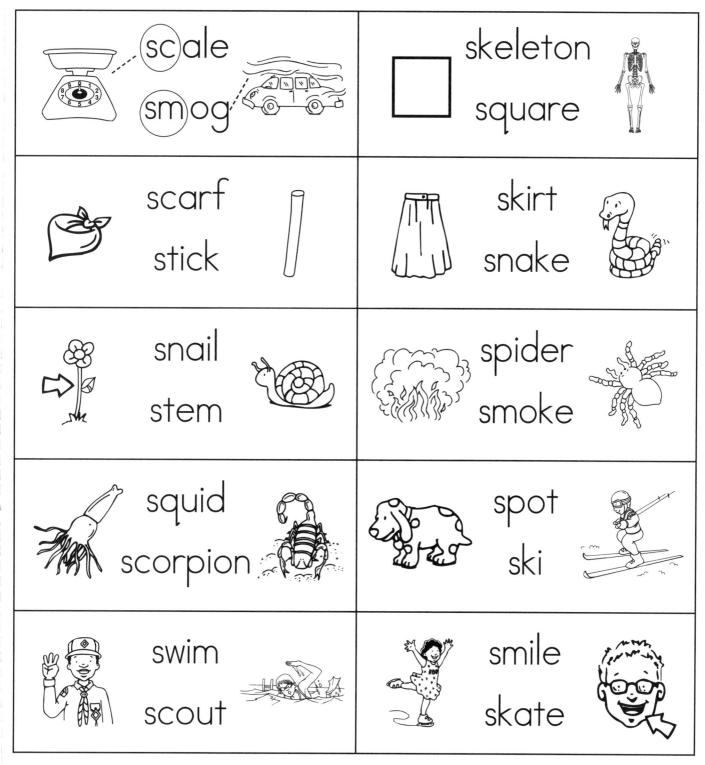

scale
smog

skeleton
square

scarf
stick

skirt
snake

snail
stem

spider
smoke

squid
scorpion

spot
ski

swim
scout

smile
skate

Initial s Clusters: *sc, sq, sh, sp, st, sm, sk, sw*

Read the words. Say each picture name. Listen for the initial *s* cluster. Write the word from the word list. Color the picture.

scone   squirrel   shop   spoon   stage   smoke   skunk   swing

scone

Read each sentence. Read the words in the word bank. Fill in the circle for the word that completes the sentence. Write that word in the sentence. Draw a picture of the sentence you just made.

The snake and the snail both had to _____.	○ sneeze ○ swim ○ sky ○ star
The scout could smell _____.	○ snack ○ smoke ○ sweat ○ camel
The spider sat on a _____.	○ smog ○ squash ○ spill ○ snow

www.summerbridgeactivities.com

Initial *s* Clusters: *sc, sn, sp, st, sm, sw, sq*

Look at each picture below. Fill in the missing letters in the word below the picture. Listen carefully for the *s* cluster sound.

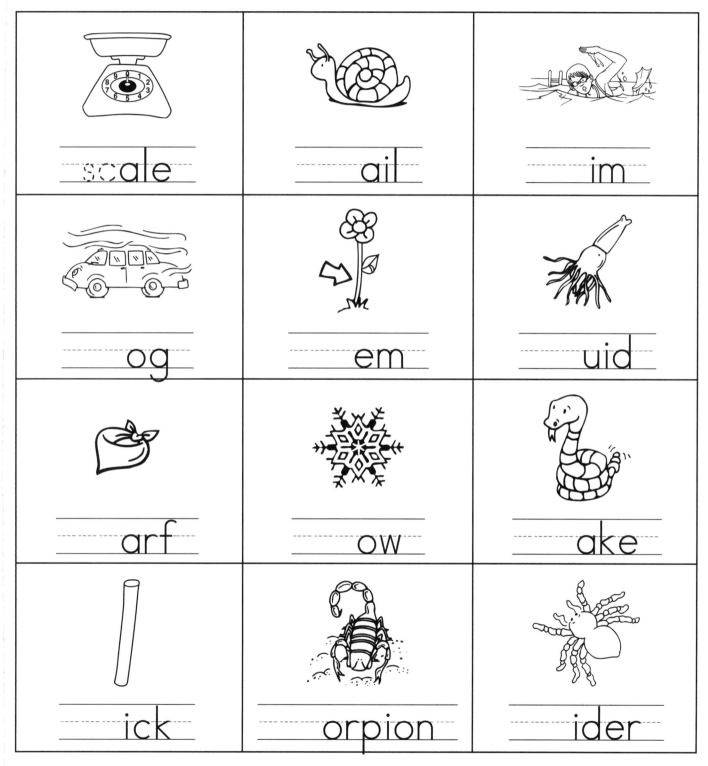

scale

___ail

___im

___og

___em

___uid

___arf

___ow

___ake

___ick

___orpion

___ider

www.summerbridgeactivities.com Phonics Connection—Grade 2—RBP0245

Initial *s* Clusters: *sc, sk, sc, sk, sn, sp, st, sm, sw, sq*

Read the story below. Say each word. Listen carefully for the *s* cluster sound. Draw a line under each word with the sound. Write your favorites in the word bank. Add to or color the picture.

A squid has eight arms. He lives in the ocean.

When he feels he is in danger,

he swims away. He also sprays ink.

He can swim very swiftly.

Squid move around in schools.

They eat snails, shrimp, crabs, and lobster.

Squid have no skeletons.

Humans can see squid when

they go diving in the ocean.

Squid can change color to help them hide.

Read each question about the story. Fill in the circle by the correct answer.

1. How many arms do squid have?

○ two   ○ four   ○ six   ○ eight

2. What do squid eat?

○ camel   ○ people   ○ shrimp   ○ ships

Write an answer.

Would you like to go diving in the ocean?

_____

On another piece of paper write how you would feel if you saw a squid in the ocean. How would you like swimming at the bottom of the ocean?

s Cluster Word Bank

squid

Name

Final *s* Clusters: *sk, sp, st*

Read the words. Say the picture names. Draw a line from each word to the picture it names. Circle the *s* cluster in each word. Color the picture.

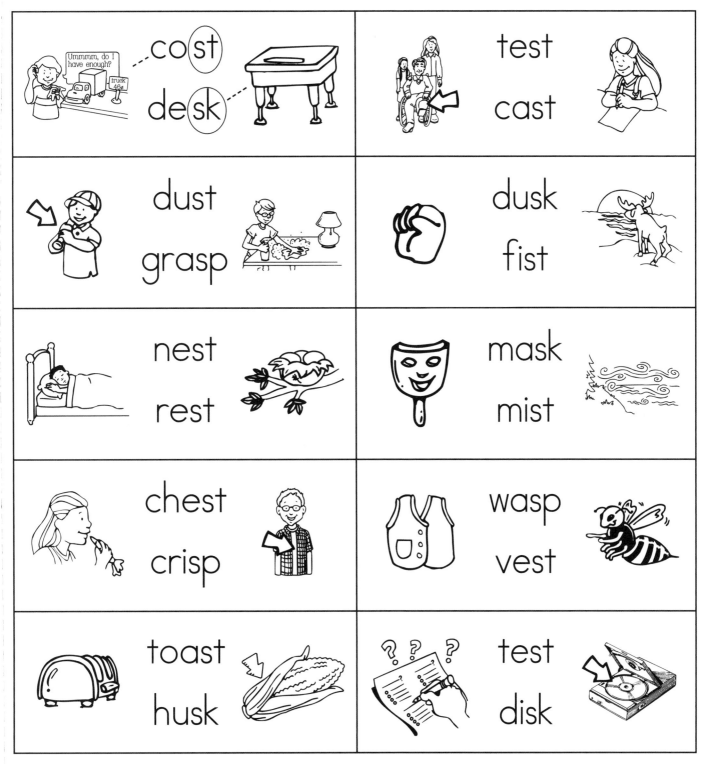

co(st)
de(sk)

test
cast

dust
grasp

dusk
fist

nest
rest

mask
mist

chest
crisp

wasp
vest

toast
husk

test
disk

73

Final s Clusters: sk, sp, st

Read the words. Say each picture name. Listen for the s cluster. Write the word from the word list. Color the picture.

toast   tusk   roast   list   husk   disk   crisp   test

toast

_____

_____

_____

_____

_____

_____

_____

Read each sentence. Read the words in the word bank. Fill in the circle for the word that completes the sentence. Write that word in the sentence. Draw a picture of the sentence you just made.

We feed the ducks _____ of bread.	○ nest ○ crusts ○ desks ○ chests
Mom made a _____ of jobs for us to do.	○ mask ○ roast ○ list ○ lost
John worked on his homework at his _____.	○ desk ○ fist ○ cost ○ rest

Name

Final s Clusters: *sk, sp, st*

Look at each picture below. Fill in the missing letters in the word below the picture. Listen carefully for the final s cluster sound.

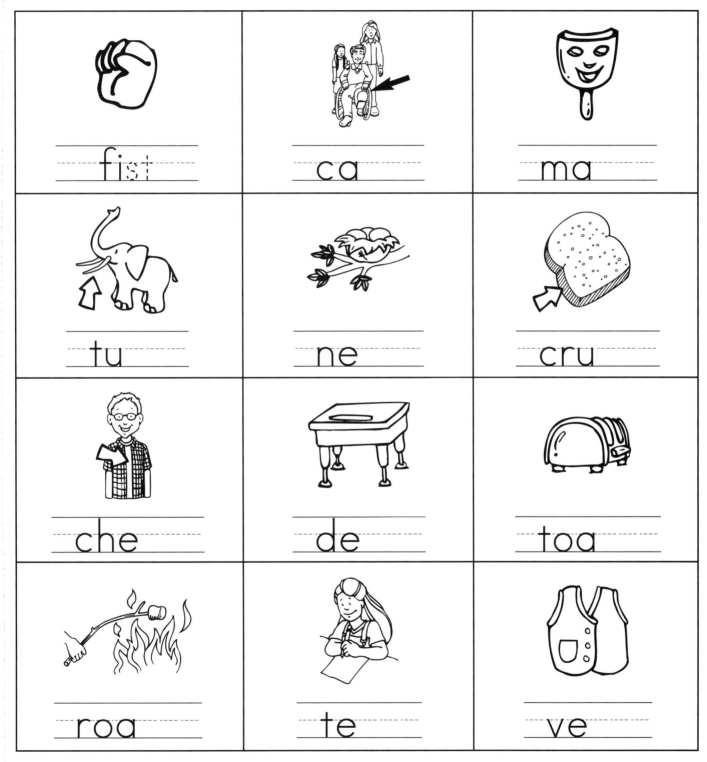

fist	ca___	ma___
tu___	ne___	cru___
che___	de___	toa___
roa___	te___	ve___

www.summerbridgeactivities.com Phonics Connection—Grade 2—RBP0245

Final s Clusters: st, sk, sp

Read the story below. Say each word. Listen carefully for the final s cluster. Draw a line under each word with a final s cluster. Write your favorites in the word bank. Add to or color the picture.

Sam and Sonny went on a scavenger hunt.

They went house to house.

They would <u>ask</u> for things on a list.

The first one who

found everything would win.

Sam had the list in his fist.

It would be a fun task.

The game was over at dusk.

Scavenger List
Halloween Mask
Bird Nest
Burnt Toast
Elephant Tusk
Small Chest
Math Test
Frozen Roast
Purple Vest

Read each question about the story. Fill in the circle by the correct answer.

1. How do you think neighbors felt when Sam and Sonny asked for things for the scavenger hunt?

   ○ happy   ○ mad   ○ sad   ○ angry

2. Do you think that Sam and Sonny won the game?

   ○ yes   ○ no

Write an answer.

Would you like to go on a scavenger hunt?

_____

_____.

On another piece of paper make a list of things you might ask for if you went on a scavenger hunt.

s Cluster
Word Bank

ask
_____
_____
_____
_____
_____
_____
_____
_____
_____
_____
_____

Initial *l* Clusters: *bl, cl, fl, gl, pl, sl*

Read the words. Say the picture names. Draw a line from each word to the picture it names. Circle the *l* clusters. Color the picture.

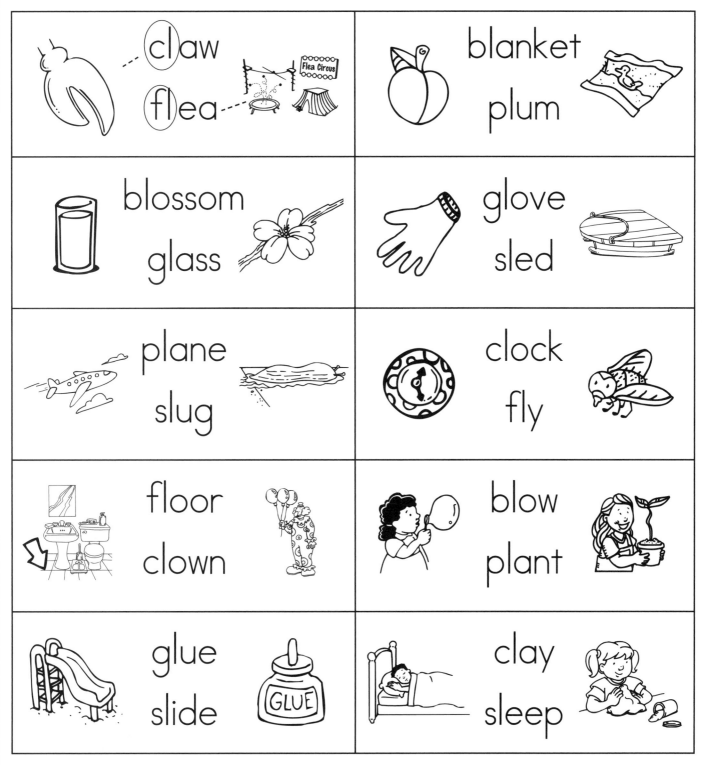

© RBP Books   www.summerbridgeactivities.com   Phonics Connection—Grade 2—RBP0245

Initial *l* Clusters: *bl, cl, fl, gl, pl, sl*

Read the words. Say each picture name. Listen for the *l* clusters. Write the word from the word list. Color the picture.

plug	block	plate	club	flag	globe	sled	slice

Read each sentence. Read the words in the word bank. Fill in the circle for the word that completes the sentence. Write that word in the sentence. Draw a picture of the sentence you just made.

Joshua plays a _____.	○ plate ○ clip ○ flute ○ block
Glen likes a _____ of milk with his cookies.	○ claw ○ glass ○ plant ○ slug
The school puts up the _____ every day.	○ blue ○ glue ○ clay ○ flag

Phonics Connection—Grade 2—RBP0245   www.summerbridgeactivities.com   ©RBP Books

Name

Initial *l* Clusters: *bl, cl, fl, gl, pl, sl*

Look at each picture below. Fill in the missing letters in the word below the picture. Listen carefully for the initial *l* cluster sound.

slug

own

ue

aw

eep

ea

ove

um

ide

ant

ay

ossom

www.summerbridgeactivities.com   Phonics Connection—Grade 2—RBP0245

Initial *l* Clusters: *bl, cl, fl, gl, pl, sl*

Read the story below. Say each word. Listen carefully for the initial *l* cluster. Draw a line under each word with an *l* cluster. Write your favorites in the word bank. Add to or color the picture.

The farmer had many things to do on the farm.
He gathered his tools.
He needed <u>pliers</u>, plugs, and plywood.
He fixed the fence with a clank, clip, and clunk.
He plowed his field with a flip, fling, and flop.
He watered the plants with a slip, slop, and splash.
He picked the plums with a plod, plump, and pluck.
He was done for the day.
He climbed into his glider and yelled, "Yipee!"

Read each question about the story. Fill in the circle by the correct answer.

1. What did the farmer not do during the day?
   ○ swim   ○ plow   ○ fix fence   ○ pick plums

2. What did he leave in at the end of the day?
   ○ plane   ○ glider   ○ tractor   ○ sled

Write an answer.

Write the names of all the tools he used.

_____

- .

On another piece of paper write some of the things you might like to do if you were on a farm.

l Cluster Word Bank

pliers

Initial *r* Clusters: *br, fr, tr, cr, gr, dr, wr, pr*

Read the words. Say the picture names. Draw a line from each word to the picture it names. Circle the *r* cluster. Color the pictures.

© RBP Books   www.summerbridgeactivities.com   Phonics Connection—Grade 2—RBP0245

Initial *r* Clusters: *br, fr, tr, cr, gr, dr, wr, pr*

Read the words. Say each picture name. Listen for the *r* clusters. Write the word from the word list. Color the picture.

frame   crow   tray   bride   grass   crib   wrist   drive

Read each sentence. Read the words in the word bank. Fill in the circle for the word that completes the sentence. Write that word in each sentence. Draw a picture of the sentence you just made.

Mom cleaned the floor with a _____ .	○ brush ○ bridge ○ broom ○ branch
We took a _____ to the mountains.	○ trash ○ treat ○ trip ○ try
The green _____ sat on a brown log.	○ freckle ○ fresh ○ fry ○ frog

Phonics Connection—Grade 2—RBP0245   ©RBP Books

Initial *r* Clusters: *br, fr, tr, cr, gr, dr, wr, pr*

Look at each picture below. Listen carefully for the *r* cluster. Fill in the missing letters in the word below the picture.

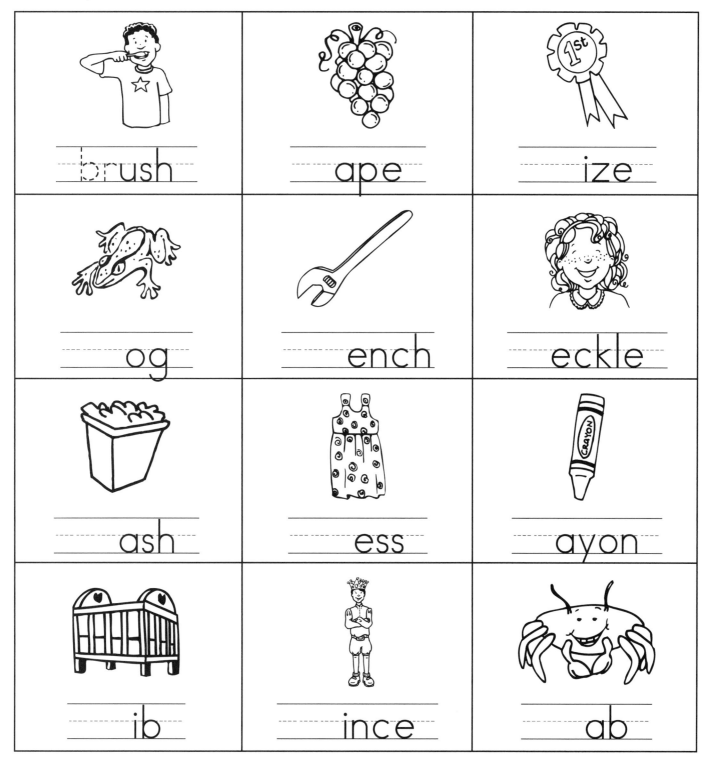

brush

ape

ize

og

ench

eckle

ash

ess

ayon

ib

ince

ab

Initial *r* Clusters: *br, fr, tr, cr, gr, dr, wr, pr*

Read the story below. Say each word. Listen for the *r* clusters. Draw a line under each word with an *r* cluster. Write your favorites in the word bank. Add to or color the picture.

A <u>frog</u> took a field trip to a school.
He met a boy with freckles named Fred.
He drew a picture with a crayon.
He won first prize for writing the best story.
At recess he hopped on the grass and ate grapes.
He drank pond water when he got thirsty.
He watched a program about a prince.
When the bell rang the teacher gave him a treat.
He hopped home to tell his mom about his
fun field day.

Read each question about the story. Fill in the circle by the correct answer.

1. What was the boy's name?
o Brad   o Fred   o Tracy   o Cream

2. How do you think the frog felt?
o scared   o happy   o worried   o sad

Write an answer.

Write some places you would like to go on a field trip.

On another piece of paper write about an experience you had on a field trip.

r Cluster
Word Bank

frog

Phonics Connection—Grade 2—RBP0245   www.summerbridgeactivities.com   ©RBP Books

Final Consonant Clusters: *ct, ft, pt, lt, lf*

Read the words. Say the picture names. Listen for the last sounds you hear. Draw a line from each word to the picture it names. Circle the final consonant cluster. Color the pictures.

li(ft)	knelt
swe(pt)	gift
wept	belt
raft	slept
left	melt
wolf	elf
wilt	quilt
shelf	golf
duct	craft
felt	soft

© RBP Books   www.summerbridgeactivities.com   Phonics Connection—Grade 2—RBP0245

Name

Final Consonant Clusters: *ct, ft, pt, lt, lf*

Read the words. Say each picture name. Listen for the final consonant clusters. Write the word from the word list. Color the picture.

swept   wilt   elf   golf   wept   raft   melt   slept

swept

Read each sentence. Read the words in the word bank. Fill in the circle for the word that completes the sentence. Write that word in the sentence. Draw a picture of the sentence you just made.

Norma got _____ clubs for her birthday.	○ elf ○ slept ○ belt ○ golf
Samantha floated down the river on a _____.	○ gift ○ quilt ○ raft ○ wolf
A baby _____ came out of the woods.	○ soft ○ fact ○ wolf ○ duct

Phonics Connection—Grade 2—RBP0245   www.summerbridgeactivities.com   © RBP Books

Name

Final Consonant Clusters: *ct, ft, pt, lt, lf*

Look at each picture below. Listen carefully for the final consonant cluster. Fill in the missing letters in the word below the picture.

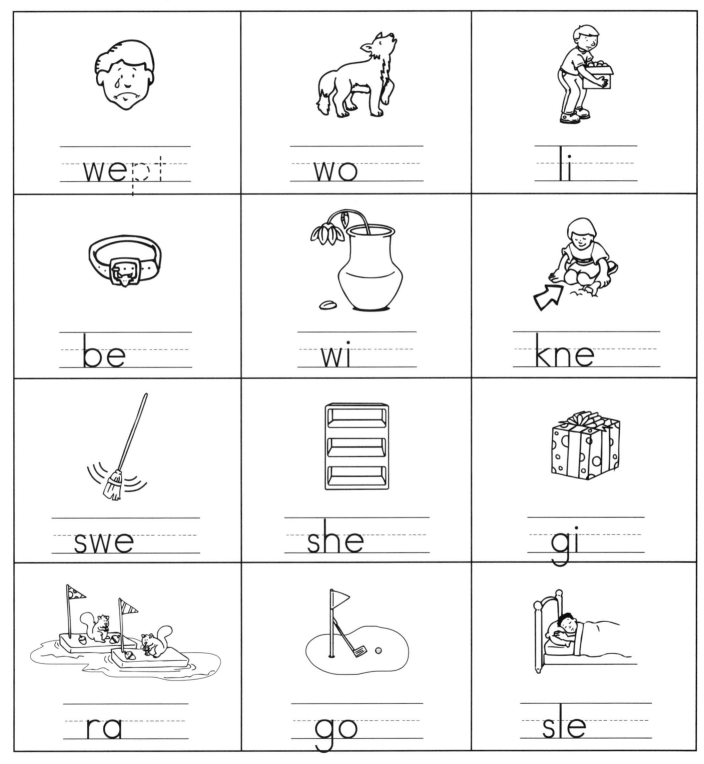

wept

wo

li

be

wi

kne

swe

she

gi

ra

go

sle

Final Consonant Clusters: *ct, ft, pt, lt, lf*

Read the story below. Say each word. Listen carefully for the sounds. Draw a line under each word with a final consonant cluster. Write your favorites in the word bank. Add to or color the picture.

Ernie the elf was glad to see the snow melt.

He wanted his friends to go down the river on a raft.

He put a quilt on the raft so they could sit.

They put the raft into the river.

As they floated they saw a wolf.

The water got swifter. It began to lift the boat.

The raft started to tilt right and left.

It felt as if they might flip over.

They were very afraid.

Read each question about the story. Fill in the circle by the correct answer.

1. What animal did they see in the woods?

    o bear   o skunk   o duck   o wolf

2. Why were the elf and his friends on the raft?

    o They wanted to float.   o There was a flood.

Write an answer.

What could they have done if the raft turned over?

_____

- -

_____

On another piece of paper write an ending to this story.

Word Bank

elf

_____

_____

_____

_____

_____

_____

_____

_____

_____

Name

Final Consonant Clusters: *nd, nk, nt, ng, mp*

Read the words. Say the picture names. Draw a line from each word to the picture it names. Circle the final consonant cluster. Color the pictures.

www.summerbridgeactivities.com Phonics Connection—Grade 2—RBP0245

Name

Final Consonant Clusters: *nd, nk, nt, mp, ng*

Read the words. Say each picture name. Listen for the final consonant clusters. Write the word from the word list. Color the picture.

stand   stamp   paint   pump   crank   cent   wind   skunk

stand   _____   _____   _____

_____   _____   _____   _____

Read each sentence. Read the words in the word bank. Fill in the circle for the word that completes the sentence. Write that word in the sentence. Draw a picture of the sentence you just made.

Spring is the time to _____ .	○ pond ○ ring ○ trunk ○ plant
Summer is when we like to _____ .	○ stamp ○ pump ○ cent ○ camp
Winter is when you find the _____ asleep in the woods.	○ skunk ○ plant ○ shrimp ○ tent

90

Final Consonant Clusters: *nd, nk, nt, mp, ng*

Look at each picture below. Listen carefully for the final consonant cluster. Fill in the missing letters in the word below the picture.

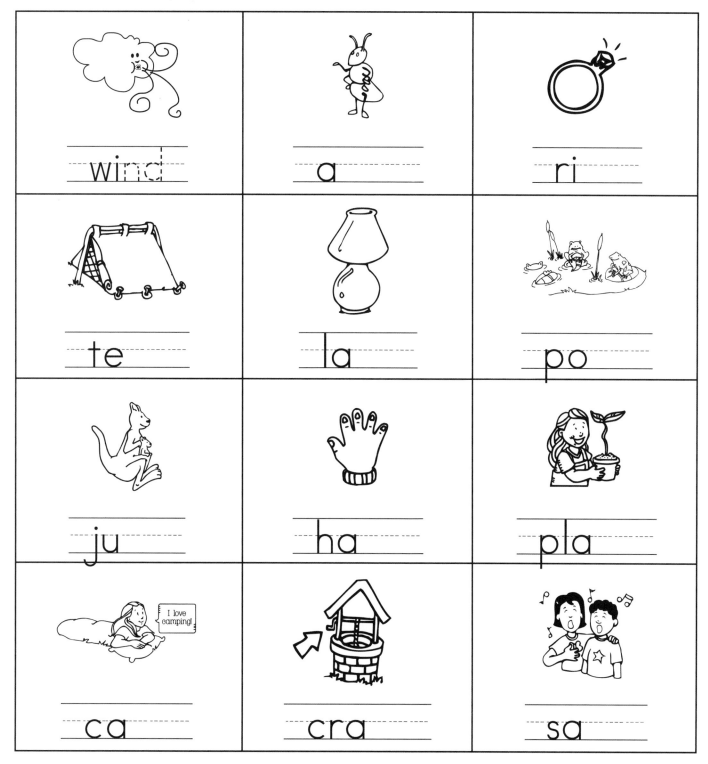

wind	a___	ri___
te___	la___	po___
ju___	ha___	pla___
ca___	cra___	sa___

Final Consonant Clusters: *nd, nk, nt, mp, ng*

Read the story below. Say each word. Listen carefully for the final consonant clusters. Draw a line under each word with a final consonant cluster. Write your favorites in the word bank. Add to or color the picture.

Every summer my family likes to <u>camp</u>.
We pack our trunk with lots of junk.
We put the fishing gear in the rear.
We drive to where the trees grow tall.
We set up the tent by the pond.
As soon as we take out the food,
the ants show up to eat!
We put worms on our hooks.
We sit on a stump waiting to catch a fish.
But watch out! There may be a skunk in that stump!

Read each question about the story. Fill in the circle by the correct answer.

Word Bank

<u>camp</u>

1. What comes into camp to eat?
   ○ dogs   ○ skunk   ○ fish   ○ ants

2. In what season do they go camping?
   ○ winter   ○ spring   ○ summer   ○ fall

Write an answer.

What does your family like to do in the summer?

_____

On another piece of paper write about an experience you had while fishing or camping.

Initial Three-Letter Clusters: *scr, str, thr, spr, spl, shr, squ*

Read the words. Say the picture names. Draw a line from each word to the picture it names. Circle the three-letter cluster. Color the pictures.

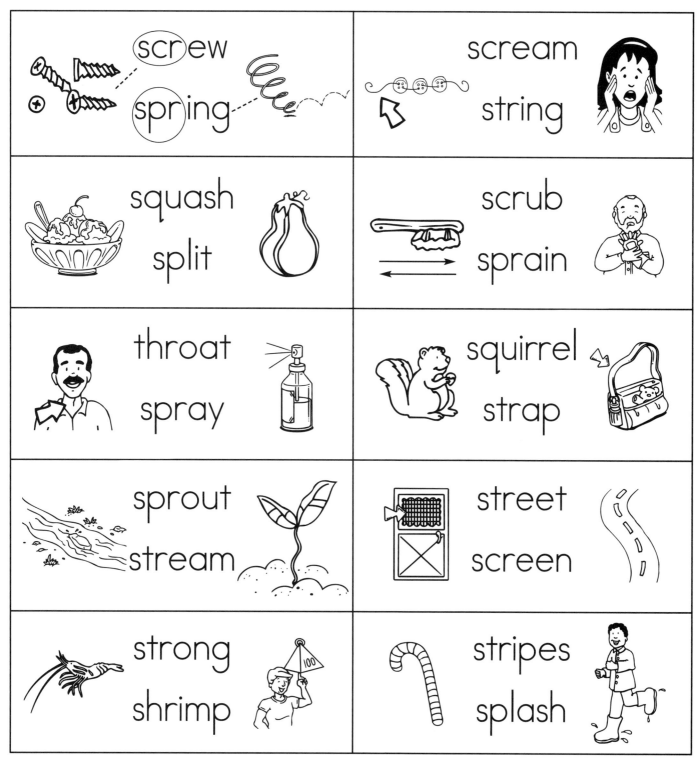

www.summerbridgeactivities.com   Phonics Connection—Grade 2—RBP0245

Initial Three-Letter Clusters: *scr, str, thr, spr, shr, sch, squ*

Read the words. Say each picture name. Listen for the initial three-letter clusters. Write the word from the word list under the picture. Color the picture.

spray   scrape   struck   school   squint   shred   three   square

Read each sentence. Read the words in the word bank. Fill in the circle for the word that completes the sentence. Write that word in the sentence. Draw a picture of the sentence you just made.

A skunk _____ in a hole in a stump.	O splashed O shrub O squids O squeezed
There are yellow _____ painted on the road.	O spring O school O stripes O three
The seal lands in the water with a big _____.	O thirsty O spring O splash O thirty

Phonics Connection—Grade 2—RBP0245   www.summerbridgeactivities.com   ©RBP Books

Initial Three-Letter Clusters: *scr, str, thr, spr, spl, squ*

Look at each picture below. Listen carefully for the initial three-letter cluster. Fill in the missing letters in the word below the picture.

scr<u>ew</u>	___ing	___ash
___ay	___out	___irrel
___eam	___ong	___int
___ipes	___ash	___oat

Initial Three-Letter Clusters: *scr, str, thr, spr, spl, sch, squ*

Read the story below. Say each word. Listen carefully for the three-letter clusters. Draw a line under each word with a three-letter cluster. Write your favorites in the word bank. Add to or color the picture.

Spring is the time to plant.
Today, we are going to plant squash.
First, you prepare the soil.
You need to be strong to turn the dirt.
Second, make a straight line with a string.
Use your hoe to follow the string to make straight rows.
Third, split the ground and put in the seed.
Fourth, spray your garden with water, or turn
a stream of water down your rows.
In 7–10 days you should see the sprouts straining
to get out of the ground and grow.

Read each question about the story. Fill in the circle by the correct answer.

1. What do you use to make a straight line?

○ shrimp   ○ screw   ○ scrub   ○ string

2. What season is the best time to plant?

○ winter   ○ spring   ○ summer   ○ fall

Write an answer.

What does a plant need to live?

_____

_____

On another piece of paper write about a seed you have planted. What happened to your plant?

Word Bank

spring

_____
_____
_____
_____
_____
_____
_____

Phonics Connection—Grade 2—RBP0245   www.summerbridgeactivities.com   ©RBP Books

Name

Final Three-Letter Clusters: *nch, dge, nce, nse, nge*

Read the words. Say the picture names. Listen to the final sounds. Draw a line from each word to the picture it names. Circle the final three-letter clusters. Color the pictures.

be(nch)

hi(nge)

lunch

fringe

bridge

pinch

crunch

lodge

pledge

branch

inch

rinse

dance

judge

fridge

prince

wrench

fudge

FUDGE 50¢

fence

bunch

97

Final Three-Letter Clusters: *nch, dge, nce, nse*

Read the words. Say each picture name. Listen for the final three-letter clusters. Write the word from the word list. Color the picture.

bench   pledge   prince   rinse   inch   fudge   fence   lunch

bench

Read each sentence. Read the words in the word bank. Fill in the circle for the word that completes the sentence. Write that word in the sentence. Draw a picture of the sentence you just made.

We say the _____ of Allegiance every day in school.	○ bench ○ hinge ○ bridge ○ pledge
The cow went through a hole in the _____.	○ fence ○ fudge ○ lodge ○ fridge
My grandpa and I sat on a _____ in the park.	○ inch ○ bench ○ dance ○ prince

Phonics Connection—Grade 2—RBP0245   ©RBP Books

Name

Final Three-Letter Clusters: *nch, dge, nce, nse, nge*

Look at each picture below. Listen carefully for the three-letter clusters. Fill in the missing letters in the word below the picture.

bench	hi ___	fu ___
bri ___	pi ___	___ u ___
fri ___	___ p l e	bra ___
da ___	___ i ___	fri ___

© RBP Books   www.summerbridgeactivities.com   Phonics Connection—Grade 2—RBP0245

Final Three-Letter Clusters: *nch, dge, nce, nse, nge*

Read the story below. Listen carefully for the final clusters. Draw a line under each word with a three-letter cluster. Write your favorites in the word bank. Add to or color the picture.

My grandma is a judge.
Today, she took me to see her work.
After work, we went to the park.
We sat on a bench.
She told me stories about a prince.
We watched people go past.
A group came over and talked
Grandma into doing a dance.
Grandma bought us each a glass of punch.
Then it was time to go home for lunch.

Read each question about the story. Fill in the circle by the correct answer.

Word Bank

judge

1. In the story, what kind of job does Grandma have?
   ○ fudge maker   ○ judge   ○ dancer   ○ prince

2. What did Grandma buy to drink?
   ○ water   ○ soda   ○ milk   ○ punch

Write an answer.

What were some of the things they did in the park?

_____

_____

On another piece of paper write about a time you went to the park. Whom did you go with? What did you see and do?

www.summerbridgeactivities.com   © RBP Books

Silent Consonants; *kn, sc, wr, gh*

Read the words. Say the picture names. Draw a line from each word to the picture it names. Circle the silent consonant clusters. Color the pictures.

Example:

The letter *k* can be silent when followed by *n*. The letter *w* can be silent when followed by *r*. The letter *c* can be silent when it follows *s*. The letter *h* can be silent when it follows *g*.

knee   wrist   scissors

Name

Silent Consonants: *kn, sc, wr, gh*

Say each picture name. Look for the silent consonant clusters. Write the word from the word list. Color the picture.

knot   wrench   scientist   knit   knock   write   knife   wrap

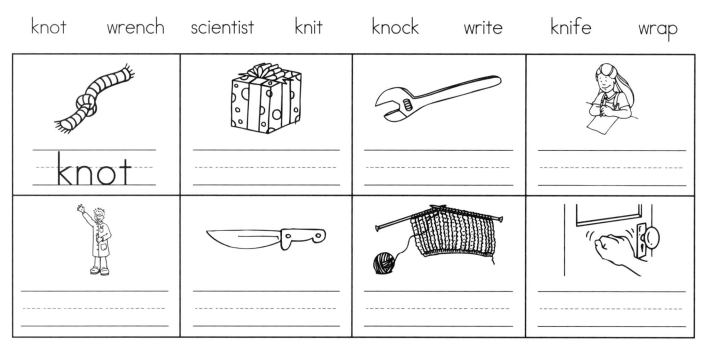

knot

Read each sentence. Read the words in the word bank. Fill in the circle for the word that completes the sentence. Write that word in the sentence. Draw a picture of the sentence you just made.

At Halloween you may see a _____.	○ ghost ○ knot
May wears a watch on her _____.	○ scared ○ wrist
Sally could smell the sweet _____ of the rose.	○ scent ○ knock
My grandpa _____ me a winter sweater.	○ scissors ○ knit

Name

Silent Consonants: *dg, gh, mb, ck*

Read the words. Say the picture names. Draw a line from each word to the picture it names. Circle the silent consonants. Color the pictures.

Example:

The letter *d* can be silent when followed by *g*. The letter *b* can be silent when it follows *m*. The letter *c* can be silent when it follows *s*. The letter *c* can be silent when followed by a *k*. The letters *gh* together can be silent when followed by *t*.

fu*d*ge   lam*b*   li*gh*t   du*c*k

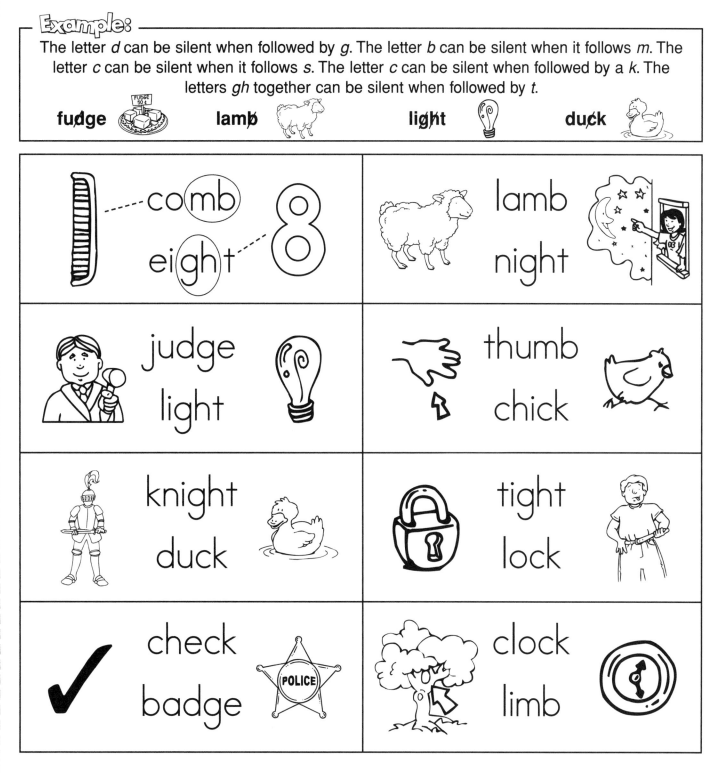

comb
eight

lamb
night

judge
light

thumb
chick

knight
duck

tight
lock

check
badge

clock
limb

www.summerbridgeactivities.com   Phonics Connection—Grade 2—RBP0245

Silent Consonants: *dg, gh, mb, ck*

Read the words. Say each picture name. Look for the silent consonant. Write the word from the word list. Color the picture.

judge   limb   night   truck   badge   light   duck   check

judge

Read each sentence. Read the words in the word bank. Fill in the circle for the word that completes the sentence. Write that word in the sentence. Draw a picture of the sentence you just made.

The lizard was on the _____.	○ rock ○ comb
Bats come out and fly at _____.	○ night ○ duck
The sheep cannot find her _____.	○ chick ○ lamb
We saw eight ducks cross a _____.	○ bridge ○ light

Phonics Connection—Grade 2—RBP0245   www.summerbridgeactivities.com   ©RBP Books

Name

Silent Consonants:

Read the story below. Say each word. Listen carefully to the sounds. Draw a line under each word with silent consonants. Write your favorites in the word bank. Add to or color the picture.

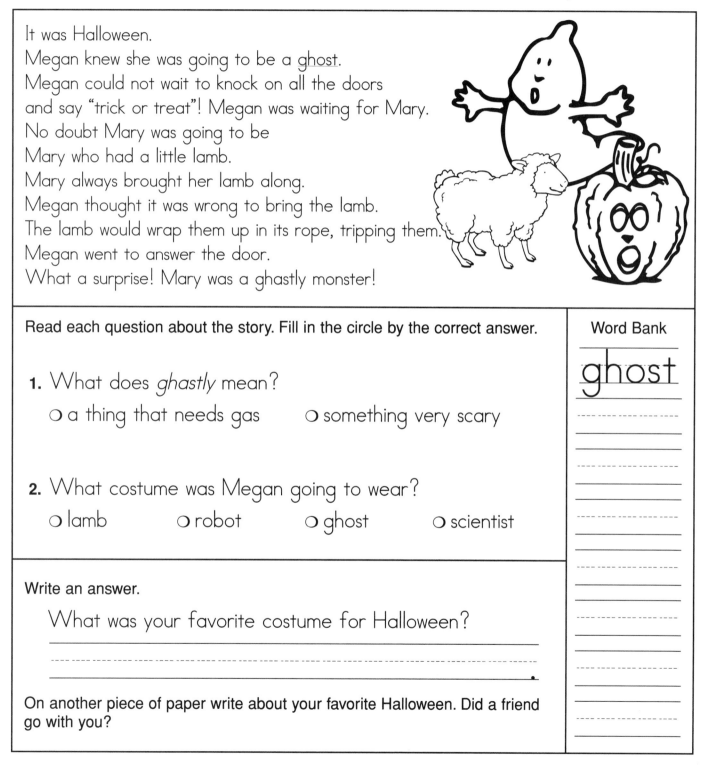

It was Halloween.
Megan knew she was going to be a ghost.
Megan could not wait to knock on all the doors
and say "trick or treat"! Megan was waiting for Mary.
No doubt Mary was going to be
Mary who had a little lamb.
Mary always brought her lamb along.
Megan thought it was wrong to bring the lamb.
The lamb would wrap them up in its rope, tripping them.
Megan went to answer the door.
What a surprise! Mary was a ghastly monster!

Read each question about the story. Fill in the circle by the correct answer.

Word Bank

ghost

1. What does *ghastly* mean?
   ○ a thing that needs gas   ○ something very scary

2. What costume was Megan going to wear?
   ○ lamb   ○ robot   ○ ghost   ○ scientist

Write an answer.

What was your favorite costume for Halloween?

_____

_____ .

On another piece of paper write about your favorite Halloween. Did a friend go with you?

©RBP Books   www.summerbridgeactivities.com   Phonics Connection—Grade 2—RBP0245

Vowels with *r: ar, or*

Read the words. Say the picture names. Draw a line from each word to the picture it names. Circle the vowel with *r*. Color the pictures.

Vowels with *r*: *ar, or*

Read the words. Say each picture name. Listen for the vowel with *r*. Write the word from the word list. Color the picture.

shark   yard   cart   horn   yarn   thorn   dart   torch

shark

Read each sentence. Read the words in the word bank. Fill in the circle for the word that completes the sentence. Write that word in the sentence. Draw a picture of the sentence you just made.

Mark will see a _____ in the ocean.	○ shark ○ horse
Bert likes to play _____.	○ darts ○ stork
Grandpa picks _____ on the farm.	○ yarn ○ corn
My dad has a very loud _____.	○ park ○ snore

© RBP Books   www.summerbridgeactivities.com   Phonics Connection—Grade 2—RBP0245

Vowels with *r*: *er*, *ir*, *ur*

Read the words. Say the picture names. Draw a line from each word to the picture it names. Circle the vowel with *r*. Color the pictures.

www.summerbridgeactivities.com

Vowels with *r*: *er, ir, ur*

Read the words. Say each picture name. Listen for the vowel with *r*. Write the word from the word list. Color the picture.

batter   curb   perm   cork   stork   stir   bird   squirt

batter

Read each sentence. Read the words in the word bank. Fill in the circle for the word that completes the sentence. Write that word in the sentence. Draw a picture of the sentence you just made.

The _____ has chicks, ducks, and pigs.	○ farmer ○ shirt ○ purse
The blue bird can sit on the _____.	○ letter ○ perch ○ jerk
The _____ can help you get well.	○ her ○ stir ○ nurse

© RBP Books   www.summerbridgeactivities.com   Phonics Connection—Grade 2—RBP0245

Name

Vowels with *r*: *er, ir, ur, ar, or*

Read the story below. Say each word. Listen carefully for vowels with the *r* sound. Draw a line under each word with a vowel with an *r* sound. Write your favorites in the word bank. Add to or color the picture.

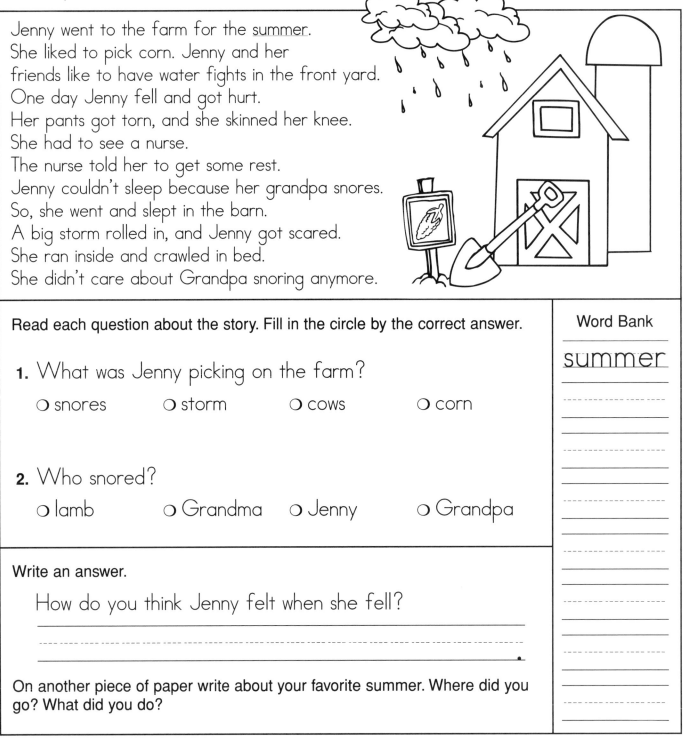

Jenny went to the farm for the <u>summer</u>.
She liked to pick corn. Jenny and her
friends like to have water fights in the front yard.
One day Jenny fell and got hurt.
Her pants got torn, and she skinned her knee.
She had to see a nurse.
The nurse told her to get some rest.
Jenny couldn't sleep because her grandpa snores.
So, she went and slept in the barn.
A big storm rolled in, and Jenny got scared.
She ran inside and crawled in bed.
She didn't care about Grandpa snoring anymore.

Read each question about the story. Fill in the circle by the correct answer.

1. What was Jenny picking on the farm?

○ snores   ○ storm   ○ cows   ○ corn

2. Who snored?

○ lamb   ○ Grandma   ○ Jenny   ○ Grandpa

Write an answer.

How do you think Jenny felt when she fell?

_____

On another piece of paper write about your favorite summer. Where did you go? What did you do?

Word Bank

summer
_____

(110)

Vowel Sound with *au, aw*

Read the words. Say the picture names. Draw a line from each word to the picture it names. Circle the vowel sound with *au* or *aw*. Color the pictures.

Example:

auto 🚗   jaw 👤

The letters *au* and *aw* can stand for the same sound.

jaw
gauze

straw
aunt

yawn
claw

auto
fawn

draw
haul

faucet
crawl

paw
laundry

sauce
lawn

www.summerbridgeactivities.com   Phonics Connection—Grade 2—RBP0245

Vowel Sound with *au, aw*

Read the words. Say each picture name. Listen for the vowel sound of *au* and *aw*. Write the word from the word list. Color the picture.

| autumn
claw | laundry
draw | daughter
jaw | shawl
sauce |

autumn

Read each sentence. Read the words in the word bank. Fill in the circle for the word that completes the sentence. Write that word in the sentence. Draw a picture of the sentence you just made.

The _____ soared high in the sky.	○ laundry ○ hawk
I like to _____.	○ gauze ○ draw
Water comes out of the _____.	○ faucet ○ paw
Write your own sentence with the *au, aw* sound. _____ _____	

Name

Vowel Sound with *oo, ew*

Read the words. Say the picture names. Draw a line from each word to the picture it names. Circle the vowel sound with *oo* or *ew*.

b(oo)t

dr(ew)

hook

flew

book

screw

tooth

news

moon

chew

spoon

crew

wood

blew

stool

threw

www.summerbridgeactivities.com

Phonics Connection—Grade 2—RBP0245

Vowels with *oo, ew*

Read the words. Say each picture name. Listen for the vowel sound of *oo* and *ew*. Write the word from the word list. Color the picture.

moose	stew	moon	screw
news	broom	blew	jewelry

moose

news

Read each sentence. Read the words in the word bank. Fill in the circle for the word that completes the sentence. Write that word in the sentence. Draw a picture of the sentence you just made.

The _____ was loose in the forest.	○ news ○ moose
Dad put a _____ in a board.	○ screw ○ moon
Mom used the _____ to clean the floor.	○ stew ○ broom
Write your own sentence with the *oo, ow* sound. _____ _____.	

www.summerbridgeactivities.com

Vowels with *au, aw, oo,* and *ew*

Read the story below. Say each word. Listen carefully for the *au, aw, oo,* and *ew* sounds. Draw a line under each word with the *au, aw, oo,* or *ew* sound. Write your favorites in the word bank. Add to or color the picture.

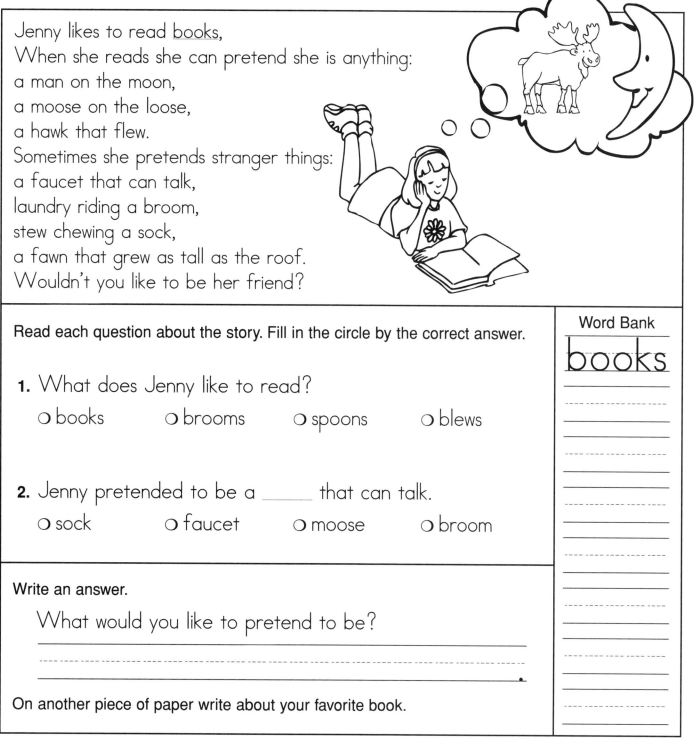

Jenny likes to read <u>books</u>,
When she reads she can pretend she is anything:
a man on the moon,
a moose on the loose,
a hawk that flew.
Sometimes she pretends stranger things:
a faucet that can talk,
laundry riding a broom,
stew chewing a sock,
a fawn that grew as tall as the roof.
Wouldn't you like to be her friend?

Read each question about the story. Fill in the circle by the correct answer.

1. What does Jenny like to read?

     ○ books   ○ brooms   ○ spoons   ○ blews

2. Jenny pretended to be a _____ that can talk.

     ○ sock   ○ faucet   ○ moose   ○ broom

Word Bank

books

Write an answer.

What would you like to pretend to be?

_____

On another piece of paper write about your favorite book.

www.summerbridgeactivities.com   Phonics Connection—Grade 2—RBP0245

Name

Diphthongs: *ou, oi, oy, ow*

Read the words. Say the picture names. Draw a line from each word to the picture it names. Circle the vowel sound with *ou, oi, oy,* or *ow.* Color the pictures.

> **Example:**
>
> The sound in the middle of *coin* is spelled by the letters *oi*. The sound in the middle of *toys* is spelled by the letters *oy*.
>
> The sound in the middle of *mouse* is spelled by the letters *ou*. The sound at the end of *cow* is spelled by the letters *ow*.

b(oy)

m(ou)ntain

soil

flower

toy

clown

boil

mouth

joy

cloud

coin

cow

Roy

towel

noise

couch

Phonics Connection—Grade 2—RBP0245   www.summerbridgeactivities.com   © RBP Books

Diphthongs: *ou, oi, oy, ow*

Read the words. Say each picture name. Listen for the vowel sounds *ou, oi, oy,* and *ow.* Write the word from the word list. Color the picture.

| gown | oyster | plow | boy |
| coin | mouse | soil | mountain |

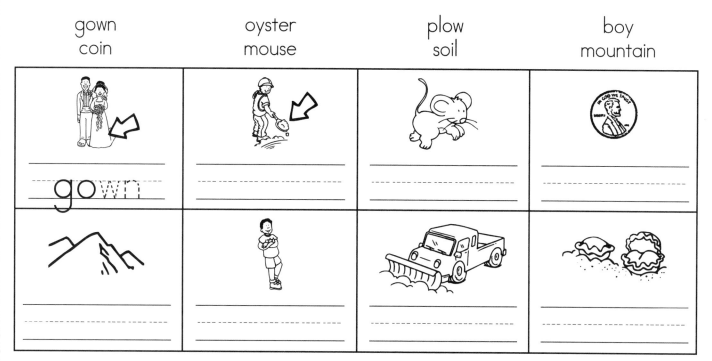

Read each sentence. Read the words in the word bank. Fill in the circle for the word that completes the sentence. Write that word in the sentence. Draw a picture of the sentence you just made.

We went downtown to see the _____.	○ clown ○ towel
Nancy has a noisy _____.	○ ploy ○ toy
The mouse ran into the _____.	○ house ○ coin
Write your own sentence with the *ou, oi, oy,* or *ow* sounds. _____ _____	

© RBP Books   www.summerbridgeactivities.com   Phonics Connection—Grade 2—RBP0245

Diphthongs: *ou, oi, oy, ow*

Read the story below. Say each word. Listen carefully for the sounds. Draw a line under each word with *ou, oi, oy,* or *ow*. Write your favorites in the word bank. Add to or color the picture.

Roy enjoyed being a cowboy.
The girls in the crowds would throw
him flowers. He rode the Brahman
bull in the rodeo. Sometimes, the
bull threw him down to the
ground. When Roy hit the ground a
cloud of soil would boil up. He would yell "ouch!"
The crowds would shout.
The clown would rush in swinging a
towel to help Roy. Roy would have to stand
up and run fast or the bull
would chase him.

Read each question about the story. Fill in the circle by the correct answer.

Word Bank

cowboy

1. Have you ever been to a rodeo?

    ○ yes   ○ no   ○ maybe

2. What sort of bull did Roy ride in the rodeo?

    ○ Brahman   ○ frogman   ○ camel   ○ clown

Write an answer.

How did Roy hit the ground when he fell off the bull?

On another piece of paper write your own story about riding in the rodeo.
Will you ride a Brahman bull or a bronco?

Root Words Ending with -ed, -ing

Read the words. Say the picture names. Add -ed or -ing to the root word. Color the pictures.

When a root word ends with one vowel followed by one consonant, double the consonant before adding -ed or -ing.

	bat	batted	batting
	fish		
	paint		
	start		
	toss		
	help		
	rub		
	miss		

Root Words Ending with *-ed, -ing*

Read the words. Say the picture names. Add *-ed* or *-ing* to the root word. Color the pictures.

When a root word ends with silent *e*, drop the *e* before adding *-ed* or *-ing*.

	bake	baked	baking
	hike		
	dance		
	use	Aaachooo!!	
	hope	I HOPE my wish comes true!	
	dine		
	carve		
	rake		

Phonics Connection—Grade 2—RBP0245   www.summerbridgeactivities.com   © RBP Books

Name

Words Ending with -ed, -ing

Read the words. Say the picture names. Add *-ed* or *-ing* to the root word. Color the pictures.

When a word ends in a consonant followed by *y*, change the *y* to *i* before adding *-ed*. When a word ends in a vowel followed by *y*, just add *-ed*. Do not change *y* before adding *-ing* to a word that ends in *y*.

	dry	dried	drying
	stay	stayed	staying
	play		
	hurry		
	cry		
	study		
	carry		
	try		

www.summerbridgeactivities.com Phonics Connection—Grade 2—RBP0245

Words Ending with -ed, -ing

Read the story below. Listen carefully for *-ed* and *-ing* word endings. Circle the correct word to make the sentence complete. Write the **root word** in the word bank. Add to or color the picture.

Linda's teacher (ask , (asked,) asking) her to do a

worksheet on words ending in –<u>ed</u> and –<u>ing</u>.

She (wish, wished, wishing) that she could visit a far away place instead.

Linda (work, worked, working) on the lesson, but pretty soon she was

(daydream, daydreamed, daydreaming).

Linda became a magician in her dream.

She (pull, pulled, pulling) a rabbit out of her hat.

The rabbit (hop, hopped, hopping) off the stage.

Read each question about the story. Fill in the circle by the correct answer.

1. What did Linda become in her daydream?

○ rabbit   ○ teacher   ○ magician   ○ student

2. What did Linda pull from her hat?

○ rabbit   ○ teacher   ○ magician   ○ student

Write an answer.

What didn't Linda want to do?

_____

_____

On another piece of paper write about a magic show. What was your favorite trick?

Root Word Bank

ask

Name

Words Ending with *-er* and *-est*

Look at the pictures. Read the words. Draw a line from each word to the picture that matches it.

The ending *-er* sometimes means "more." For example, *smaller* means "more small." The ending *-est* means "most." For example, *smallest* means "most small."

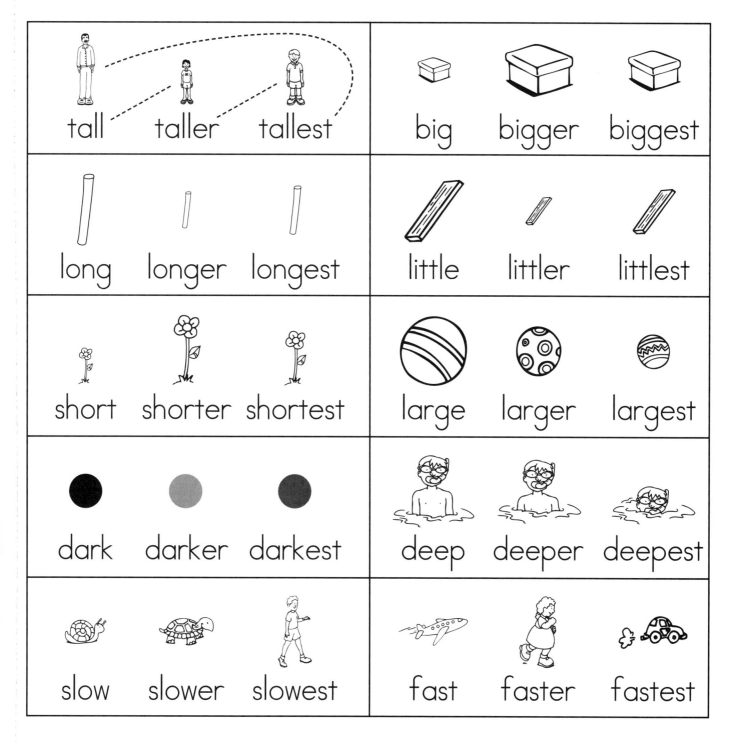

www.summerbridgeactivities.com   **Phonics Connection—Grade 2—RBP0245**

Words Endings with *-er* and *-est*

Read the words. Say each picture name. Listen for the words ending with *-er* and *-est*. Write the word from the word list under the picture. Color the picture.

tallest   deepest   smaller   longest
shorter   larger   faster   older

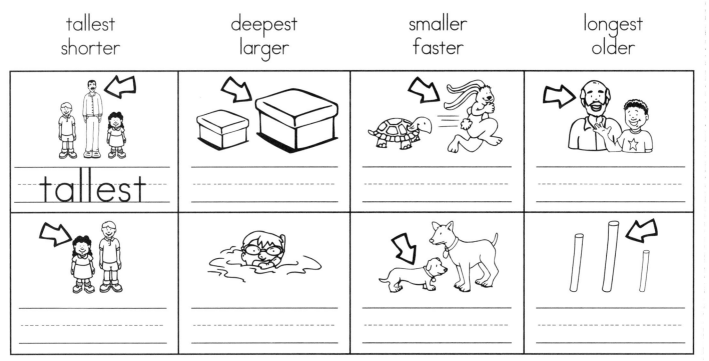

tallest

Read each sentence. Read the words in the word bank. Fill in the circle for the word that completes the sentence. Write that word in the sentence. Draw a picture of the sentence you just made.

The pine tree was _____ than the house.	○ tall ○ taller ○ tallest
Brooke's hair is _____ than yours.	○ light ○ lighter ○ lightest
My present was the _____.	○ large ○ larger ○ largest

Phonics Connection—Grade 2—RBP0245   www.summerbridgeactivities.com   ©RBP Books

Words Ending with -er and -est

Read the story. Listen carefully for -ed and -ing word endings. Circle the correct word to make the sentence complete. Write the **root word** in the word bank. Add to or color the picture.

The (old, older, (oldest)) lady on the block
lived in the (small, smaller, smallest) house.
She had the (loud, louder, loudest) dog
you ever heard. She had the (sweet, sweeter, sweetest)
smelling flowers you ever smelled.
Her yellow blouse was so (bright, brighter, brightest)
you could lose your sight. Her homemade
stew was (tasty, tastier, tastiest) than most.
Her old hands were (rough, rougher, roughest),
and her touch was scratchy. She was the
(nice, nicer, nicest) old lady on the block.

Read each question about the story. Fill in the circle by the correct answer.

Root Word Bank

old

1. What kind of house did the old lady live in?
   - ○ small
   - ○ smaller
   - ○ smallest

2. How loud was her dog?
   - ○ loud
   - ○ louder
   - ○ loudest

Write an answer.

Why do you think the old lady's hands were rough?

_____

_____.

On another piece of paper write a story about your grandmother or grandfather. Where do they live? What you do when you go there?

www.summerbridgeactivities.com Phonics Connection—Grade 2—RBP0245

Plurals: -s, -es

Read the word. Say the picture name. Draw a line from each word to the picture it names. Circle the -s or -es in the plural form of the word. Color the picture.

You can make many words mean "more than one" by adding -s or -es to base words. When a word ends in s, ss, sh, ch, or x you need to add -es to make it mean "more than one."

Example:

dresses   dishes   boxes

bird
birds

lid
lids

jet
jets

bus
buses

peach
peaches

pine
pines

hand
hands

cake
cakes

www.summerbridgeactivities.com   © RBP Books

Plurals: -s, -es

Read the words. Say each picture name. Make each word plural by adding -s or -es. Color the picture.

cap	hut	top	pig
cube	kite	rope	cake

caps

Read each sentence. Read the words in the word bank. Fill in the circle for the word that completes the sentence. Write that word in the sentence. Draw a picture of the sentence you just made.

Matt likes to eat _____.	○ peach ○ peaches
Three _____ went swimming.	○ duck ○ ducks
I washed both of my _____.	○ hands ○ hand
I missed the school _____.	○ bus ○ buses

© RBP Books   www.summerbridgeactivities.com   Phonics Connection—Grade 2—RBP0245

Plurals: -s, -es, -ies

Read the word. Say the picture name. Draw a line from each word to the picture it names. Circle the -s, -es, or -ies in the plural form of the word. Color the picture.

When a word ends in a consonant followed by a *y*, change the *y* to *i* and add -es to make it mean "more than one." When a word ends in a vowel followed by *y*, just add -s.

Example:

story   stories

boy   boys

baby

bab(ies)

book

books

key

keys

watch

watches

pony

ponies

frog

frogs

bunny

bunnies

daisy

daisies

N<mark>ame</mark>

Plurals: -s, -es, -ies

Read the words. Say each picture name. Make each word plural by adding -s or -ies. Write the word from the word list under the picture. Color the picture.

| story | penny | baby | tray |
| bunny | boy | pony | daisy |

stories

Read each sentence. Read the words in the word bank. Fill in the circle for the word that completes the sentence. Write that word in the sentence. Draw a picture of the sentence you just made.

The _____ were crying all night long.	○ baby ○ babies
The _____ were hopping in the field.	○ bunny ○ bunnies
Four _____ joined a band.	○ boy ○ boys
My mom gave me ten _____.	○ penny ○ pennies

Plurals: -s, -es

Read the story. Underline the words in plural form. Write the root word in the word bank. Add to or color the picture.

Frogs live almost everywhere.
Frogs live in ponds, marshes, and ditches.
The largest frog is eight inches long and
weighs one and one-half pounds. They come
in many colors: green, yellow, blue, and red.
Frogs eat insects like flies.
Frog babies are tadpoles. The babies
use gills to breathe. During their first
ten weeks they grow legs and lungs and
lose their tails. Then, they hop on
land and start croaking. Their chorus
of croaks sounds like motorcycles roaring.

Read each question about the story. Fill in the circle by the correct answer.

Root Word Bank

frog

1. What sounds do frogs make?
   ○ croaking   ○ jumping   ○ swimming

2. What size is the largest frog?
   ○ four inches   ○ six inches   ○ eight inches

Write an answer.

Frogs start out as tadpoles. How are tadpoles different
from frogs? _____.

On another piece of paper write a story about a pet frog. What kind of home would you build for the frog? Where would you take your frog?

Possessive: 's

Read the word. Say the picture name. Draw a line from each word to the picture it names. Circle the possessive form of the word. Color the picture.

To show that something belongs to a person or thing, add 's to the end of the word that names the owner.

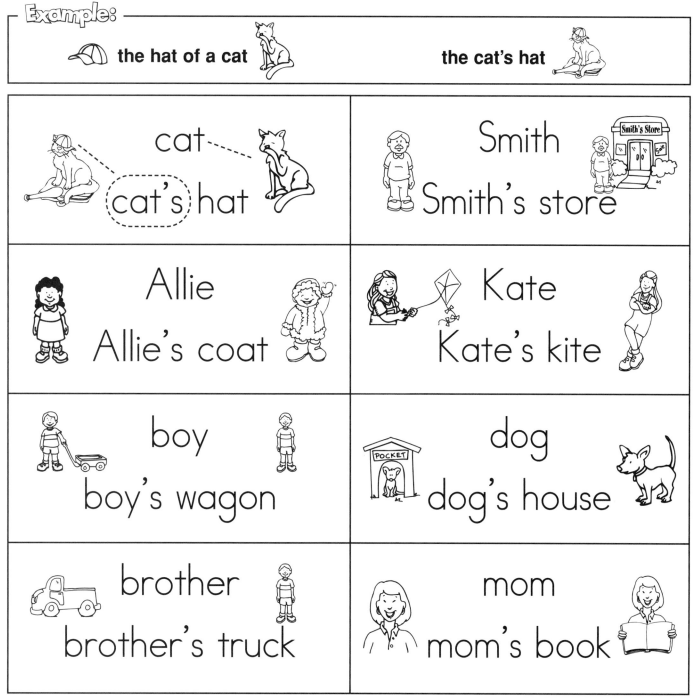

Example:

the hat of a cat

the cat's hat

cat

cat's hat

Smith

Smith's store

Allie

Allie's coat

Kate

Kate's kite

boy

boy's wagon

dog

dog's house

brother

brother's truck

mom

mom's book

www.summerbridgeactivities.com Phonics Connection—Grade 2—RBP0245

Possessive: 's

Read the words. Say each picture name. Write the word in possessive form (*duck* → *duck's*). Color the picture.

Read each sentence. Read the words in the word bank. Fill in the circle for the word that completes the sentence. Write that word in the sentence. Draw a picture of the sentence you just made.

A toy that belongs to the cat is the _____ toy.	○ cat ○ cat's
The dog that belongs to Tanner is _____ dog.	○ Tanner ○ Tanner's
My mom gave me ten _____.	○ penny ○ pennies
I eat my school lunch on a _____.	○ tray ○ trays

Phonics Connection—Grade 2—RBP0245   www.summerbridgeactivities.com   © RBP Books

Possessive: 's

Read the story below. Say each word. Look carefully for the possessive form. Draw a line under each word in the possessive form. Write the word in the word bank. Add to or color the picture.

Jerry sat down to write a story. He sat at his dad's desk. He typed on his mother's computer. He wore his brother's slippers. His dog was chewing on a toy. His dog's toy kept squeaking. Jerry got up to let the dog out. He tripped on his sister's skateboard. He looked outside to gather his thoughts and saw the snowman's head was falling off. It looked like such a nice day he went to play.

Read each question about the story. Fill in the circle by the correct answer.

1. What was Jerry working on?

○ writing a story   ○ fixing a computer

2. Whose slippers was he wearing?

○ his brother's   ○ his dad's   ○ his mother's

Write an answer.

What kept Jerry from writing his story?

_____

_____

On another piece of paper write about a time you could not finish something because of things that happened.

Word Bank

dad's

_____

_____

_____

_____

_____

_____

_____

_____

© RBP Books   www.summerbridgeactivities.com   Phonics Connection—Grade 2—RBP0245

Contractions: '*ll*

A contraction is made by putting two words together to make one shorter word. An apostrophe (') takes the place of the letter or letters that are left out.

I (wi)ll → I'll   you (wi)ll → you'll

Read the words. Draw a line from the two words to the contraction that means the same thing.

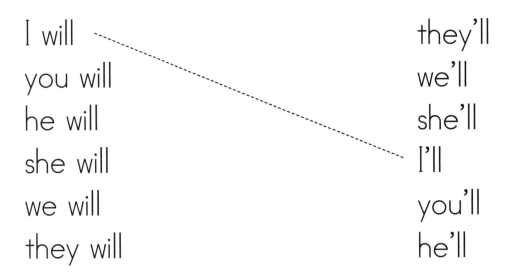

I will   they'll
you will   we'll
he will   she'll
she will   I'll
we will   you'll
they will   he'll

Read the words below. Print the contraction for the words. Write a sentence using the contraction.

I will	I'll	I'll see you tomorrow.
you will		
he will		
she will		
we will		

Phonics Connection—Grade 2—RBP0245   www.summerbridgeactivities.com   ©RBP Books

Contractions: 've, 's

A contraction is made by putting two words together to make one shorter word. An apostrophe (') takes the place of the letter or letters that are left out.

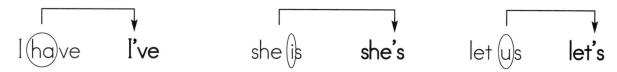

I (ha)ve → I've   she (i)s → she's   let (u)s → let's

Read the words. Draw a line from the two words to the contraction that means the same thing.

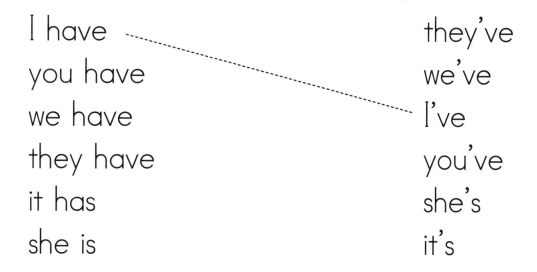

I have	they've
you have	we've
we have	I've
they have	you've
it has	she's
she is	it's

Read the words below. Print the contraction for the words. Write a sentence using the contraction.

I have   I've   I've seen a green snake.

you have

we have

it has

she is

© RBP Books   www.summerbridgeactivities.com   Phonics Connection—Grade 2—RBP0245

Contractions: 're, 's, 'm

A contraction is made by putting two words together to make one shorter word. An apostrophe (') takes the place of the letter or letters that are left out.

I am   I'm   he is   he's   we are   we're

Read the words. Draw a line from the two words to the contraction that means the same thing.

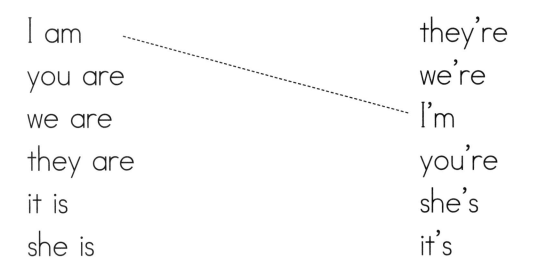

I am	they're
you are	we're
we are	I'm
they are	you're
it is	she's
she is	it's

Read the words below. Print the contraction for the words. Write a sentence using the contraction.

I am	I'm	I'm going to eat dinner.
you are		
we have		
they are		
it is		

www.summerbridgeactivities.com   © RBP Books

Name

Contractions: 't

A contraction is made by putting two words together to make one shorter word. An apostrophe (') takes the place of the letter or letters that are left out.

has n⊙t   **hasn't**   could n⊙t   **couldn't**

Read the words. Draw a line from the words to the contraction that means the same thing.

have not	hasn't	cannot	shouldn't
has not	hadn't	could not	can't
had not	haven't	should not	couldn't
do not	didn't	is not	aren't
did not	doesn't	are not	wasn't
does not	don't	was not	isn't

Read the contractions below. Print the words. Write a sentence using the contraction.

haven't   have   not   I haven't read the book.

weren't

didn't

isn't

won't

Name

Contractions

Read the letter. Say each word. Write the proper contraction for the words in parentheses on the line above them.

April 12, 2003

Dear Sam,

_____ sorry. I _____ play with you today. I
   (I am)   (cannot)

_____ listen to my Mom. My Mom said, "_____
  (did not)   (Do not)

jump on the bed." I _____ listening to her.
                      (was not)

_____ all my fault I broke my leg. _____ be
  (It is)   (We will)

going to the doctor soon. _____ need to put a cast on my
                         (He will)

leg. _____ never had a cast before. _____
    (I have)   (You will)

write your name on my cast, _____ you?
                          (will not)

Love,

Abbie

On another sheet of paper write a letter to a friend. Try to use as many contractions as you can.

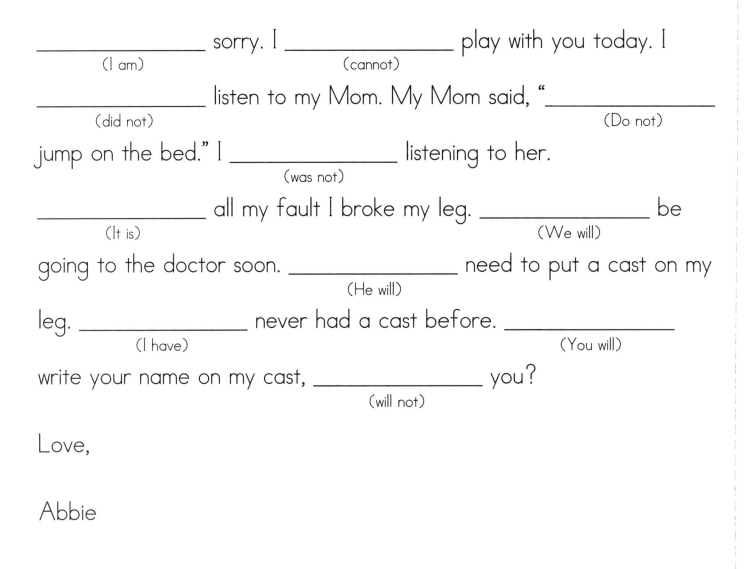

138

Compound Words

Look at the pictures. Write the two words that make up each compound. Write the compound word.

Example:

A compound word is a word made up of two smaller words.

butter + fly = butterfly

www.summerbridgeactivities.com

Phonics Connection—Grade 2—RBP0245

Name

Compound Words

Look at the pictures. Write the two words that make up each compound. Write the compound word.

Example: fire + man = fireman

Phonics Connection—Grade 2—RBP0245 www.summerbridgeactivities.com ©RBP Books

Name

Compound Words

Read the words below. Draw a line from the simple words to the compound word they make.

A compound word is a word made up of two smaller words.

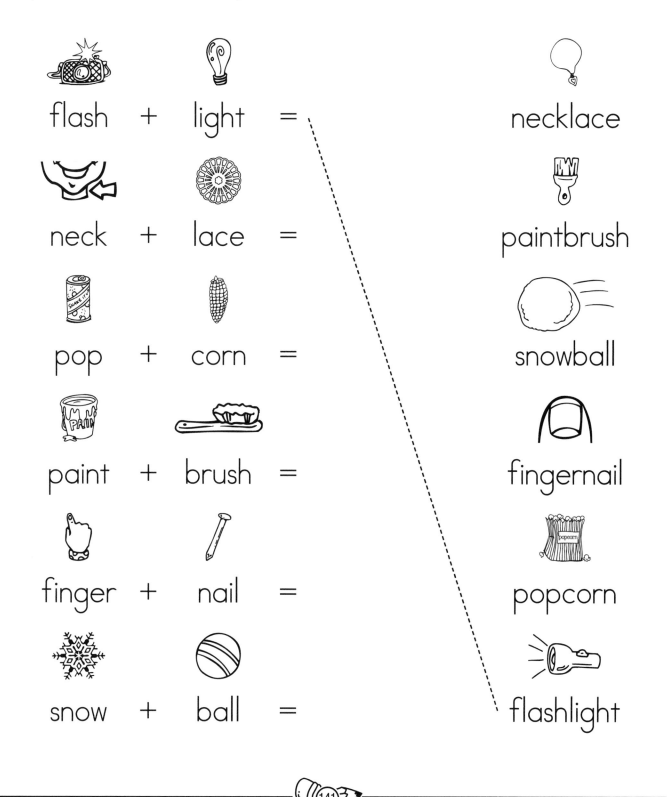

flash + light =   necklace

neck + lace =   paintbrush

pop + corn =   snowball

paint + brush =   fingernail

finger + nail =   popcorn

snow + ball =   flashlight

© RBP Books   www.summerbridgeactivities.com   Phonics Connection—Grade 2—RBP0245

Compound Words

Read the story below. Look carefully for the compound words. Draw a line under each compound word. Write your favorites in the word bank. Add to or color the picture.

Dear Mom and Dad,

I went to the <u>barnyard</u> yesterday and saw the pigpen. The pigs' pigtails twitch and wiggle. Grandpa and I took the toolbox and fixed the doghouse. Then we fixed the clothesline. We saw a bluebird by the railroad tracks. Grandma made pancakes and eggs for breakfast. Grandma did not need a cookbook. After breakfast, we painted the rowboat. There was a rainbow today. I love the farm.

Love,
Mike

Word Bank

barnyard

Read each question about the story. Fill in the circle by the correct answer.

1. Where did Mike see the pigs?

    ○ pigpen   ○ doghouse   ○ railroad

2. What did Grandma fix for breakfast?

    ○ pig slop   ○ pancakes   ○ chicken feed

Write an answer.

Mike and Grandpa painted the _____.

On another piece of paper write a letter to your mom and dad about things you would like to do on a farm.

Name

Syllables

Say the words below. Listen for the vowel sounds. Print the number of syllables on the lines.

Example:

All words are made up of one or more parts. Each part is called a syllable.
Each syllable has a separate vowel sound.

1 vowel sound
1 syllable — fox

2 vowel sounds
2 syllables — bas · ket

dog 1

rabbit 2

rope ___

dragon ___

rake ___

bat ___

rocket ___

seven ___

pillow ___

mouth ___

skunk ___

bathtub ___

chick ___

wagon ___

bed ___

bird ___

www.summerbridgeactivities.com

Phonics Connection—Grade 2—RBP0245

Name

Syllables

Read the words. They are two-syllable words. Mark the vowel sound for each syllable. The first two are done for you.

răb/bĭt	mŏn/kēy	ti/ger	ba/boon
bea/ver	bull/frog	liz/ard	cat/fish
chip/munk	dol/phin	fire/fly	ger/bil
tur/tle	blue/bīrd	le/mur	man/tis

Phonics Connection—Grade 2—RBP0245

www.summerbridgeactivities.com

©RBP Books

Homophones

Read the words. Look carefully at the spelling. Say the picture name. Draw a line from each word to the picture it names. Color the picture.

Words that are pronounced the same but have different meanings and spellings are called homophones.

www.summerbridgeactivities.com
Phonics Connection—Grade 2—RBP0245

Homophones

Read the words. Say each picture name. Write the word from the word list. Color the picture.

ring	sail	wring	sale
rode	son	sun	road

ring

wring

Read each sentence. Read the words in the word bank. Fill in the circle for the word that completes the sentence. Write that word in the sentence. Draw a picture of the sentence you just made.

Jane _____ out the candles.	○ blew ○ blue
We can _____ at the lake.	○ sail ○ sale
I _____ in my new car.	○ road ○ rode
The _____ stung me.	○ bee ○ be

Homophones

Dear Ant,

I wood like you two come to my bawl game. It is in a weak. We play on Monday knight. It will bee a grate game. You will yell so loud that you will become horse. I maid you a special surprise. Hope to sea you soon.

Love,

Brooke

Write the note again using the correct homophones:

ball   would   be   great hoarse see   week   to   made Aunt night

_____

_____

_____

_____

_____

_____

_____

_____

_____

_____

_____

_____

_____

Write your own note to someone. Write in the wrong homophones. Exchange it with a classmate and see if they can rewrite the correct homophones.

Antonyms

Read the words. Look carefully at the spelling. Say the picture name. Draw a line from each word to the picture it names. Color the picture.

Example:

An antonym is a word that has the opposite meaning of another word.

yes – no   happy – sad

thin

thick

in

out

fast

slow

sleep

awake

light

dark

hot

cold

sit

stand

hard

soft

Antonyms

Read the words. Say each picture name. Write the word from the word list. Color the picture.

sick	frown	girl	well
stand	sit	smile	boy

Read each sentence. Read the words in the word bank. Fill in the circle for the word that completes the sentence. Write that word in the sentence. Draw a picture of the sentence you just made.

Jane did not feel well; she was _____ .	○ well ○ sick
Fish swim _____ water.	○ over ○ under
Jim's TV show comes _____ *Barney* and before *Batman*.	○ before ○ after
The day is light, and the night is _____ .	○ light ○ dark

www.summerbridgeactivities.com   Phonics Connection—Grade 2—RBP0245

Antonyms

Read the story. Replace the underlined word with an antonym. Write the new word in the word bank. Reread the story. Add to or color the picture.

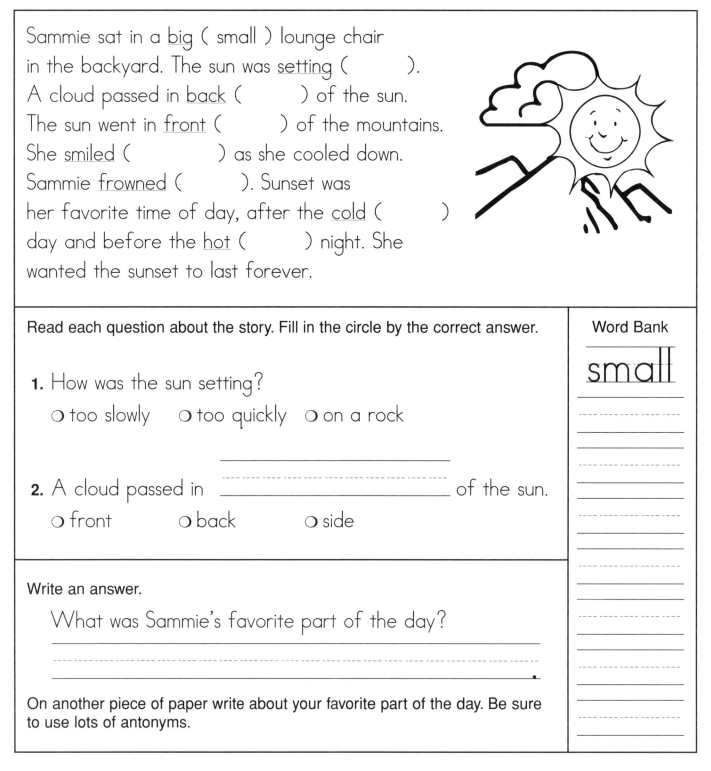

Sammie sat in a big (small) lounge chair
in the backyard. The sun was setting (   ).
A cloud passed in back (   ) of the sun.
The sun went in front (   ) of the mountains.
She smiled (   ) as she cooled down.
Sammie frowned (   ). Sunset was
her favorite time of day, after the cold (   )
day and before the hot (   ) night. She
wanted the sunset to last forever.

Read each question about the story. Fill in the circle by the correct answer.

Word Bank

small

1. How was the sun setting?
   ○ too slowly   ○ too quickly   ○ on a rock

   _____

2. A cloud passed in _____ of the sun.
   ○ front   ○ back   ○ side

Write an answer.

What was Sammie's favorite part of the day?

_____

_____.

On another piece of paper write about your favorite part of the day. Be sure to use lots of antonyms.

Phonics Connection—Grade 2—RBP0245   www.summerbridgeactivities.com   © RBP Books

Name

Synonyms

Read the words. Look carefully at the spelling. Say the picture name. Draw a line from the picture to the words that name it. Color the picture.

Example:

A synonym is a word that has the same or nearly the same meaning as another.

small – little

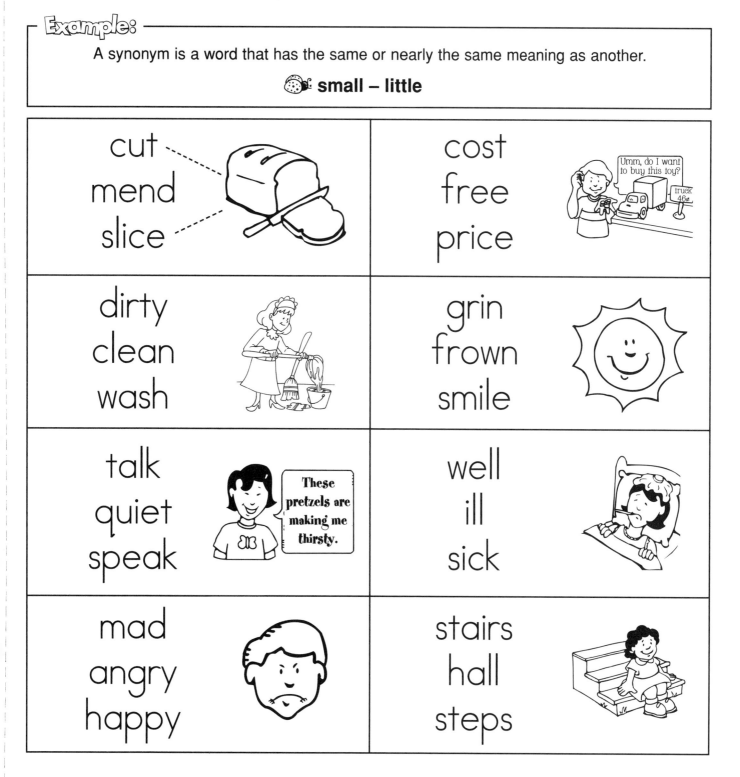

cut
mend
slice

cost
free
price

Umm, do I want to buy this toy?

truck 46¢

dirty
clean
wash

grin
frown
smile

talk
quiet
speak

These pretzels are making me thirsty.

well
ill
sick

mad
angry
happy

stairs
hall
steps

www.summerbridgeactivities.com

Phonics Connection—Grade 2—RBP0245

Name

Synonyms

Read the story. Look at the underlined words. Write a synonym for each underlined word in the word bank. Add to or color the picture.

Allie ran up the <u>steps</u> and <u>yelled</u>, "Mom, my bike is on sale!" She was so happy she could not <u>talk</u> softly. It was a <u>lovely</u> bike. Now she could afford the price of the bike. She was so excited she forgot to <u>shut</u> the door. Her mother told her to wash her face and hands. Her mother said it was a good thing Allie had <u>saved</u> her money. She would be <u>sad</u> if she still could not buy the bike. Allie had a big <u>smile</u> on her face.

Read each question about the story. Fill in the circle by the correct answer.

1. Allie saved her money because she wanted to buy a bike. What is another word for <u>saved</u>?

    ○ kept   ○ spent   ○ hid   ○ hide

2. The bike Allie wanted was pretty. What is another word for <u>pretty</u>?

    ○ lovely   ○ ugly   ○ short   ○ clean

Word Bank

stairs

_____

_____

_____

_____

_____

_____

_____

Write an answer.

Why was Allie so happy?

_____

_____

On another piece of paper rewrite the story replacing the underlined words with the words from the word bank.

Phonics Connection—Grade 2—RBP0245   www.summerbridgeactivities.com   © RBP Books

Name

ABC Order

Fill in the circle for **yes** if the words are in ABC order. Fill in the circle for **no** if the words are not in ABC order.

ape bat cat ○ yes ○ no	fox elk gerbil ○ yes ○ no	lion mole ox ○ yes ○ no
whale yak zebra ○ yes ○ no	monkey pig goat ○ yes ○ no	deer hamster kangaroo ○ yes ○ no
anteater giraffe tiger ○ yes ○ no	rabbit sheep wolf ○ yes ○ no	baboon elephant donkey ○ yes ○ no
skunk moose bear ○ yes ○ no	seal porcupine hippo ○ yes ○ no	alligator camel otter ○ yes ○ no

ABC Order

Write the words in ABC order.

apple fig banana	carrot squash onion
pear lime grape	corn beets lettuce
melon peach cherry	spinach cabbage potato

Name

ABC Order

Read the story below. Say each word.

Your mom has made you a list of groceries. She needs you to go get them.  She says it is easiest if you put them in ABC order. The store has them on their shelves in that order. This way it won't take you so long. Put the items on the list in ABC order.

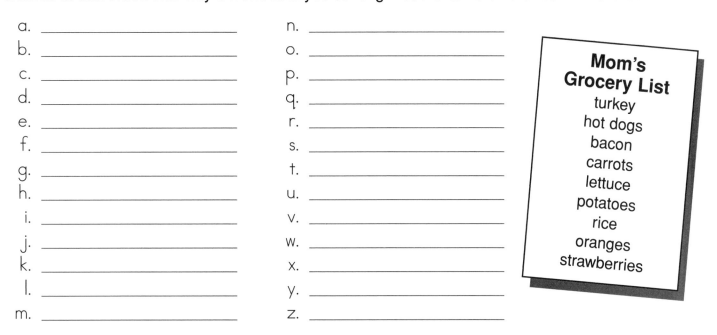

a. _____
b. _____
c. _____
d. _____
e. _____
f. _____
g. _____
h. _____
i. _____
j. _____
k. _____
l. _____
m. _____

n. _____
o. _____
p. _____
q. _____
r. _____
s. _____
t. _____
u. _____
v. _____
w. _____
x. _____
y. _____
z. _____

Mom's Grocery List
turkey
hot dogs
bacon
carrots
lettuce
potatoes
rice
oranges
strawberries

Write the names of all the students in your class in ABC order. There may be two or more names on one letter.

a. _____
b. _____
c. _____
d. _____
e. _____
f. _____
g. _____
h. _____
i. _____
j. _____
k. _____
l. _____
m. _____

n. _____
o. _____
p. _____
q. _____
r. _____
s. _____
t. _____
u. _____
v. _____
w. _____
x. _____
y. _____
z. _____

www.summerbridgeactivities.com **Phonics Connection—Grade 2—RBP0245**

Answer Pages

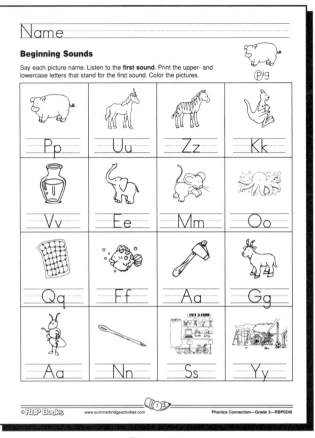

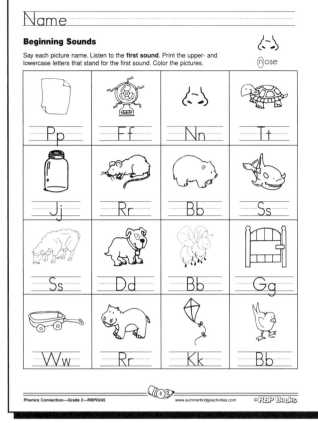

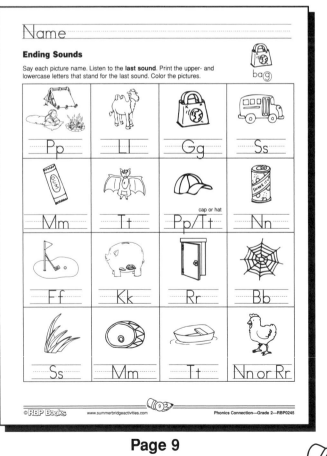

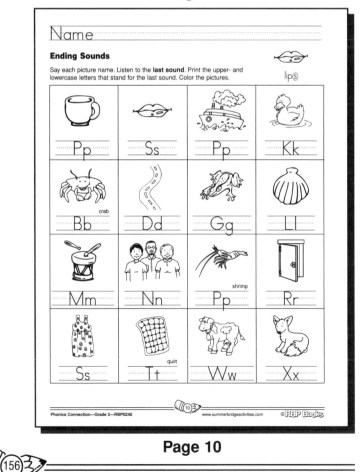

Page 7

Page 8

Page 9

Page 10

Answer Pages

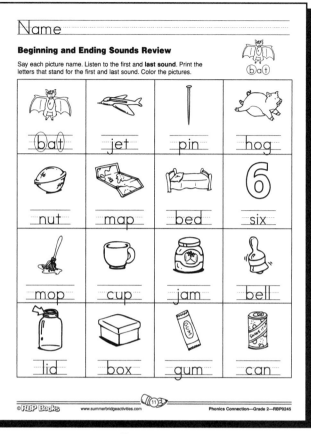

Page 11

Name

Beginning and Ending Sounds Review

Say each picture name. Listen to the first and last sound. Print the letters that stand for the first and last sound. Color the pictures.

b(a)t

bat	jet	pin	hog
nut	map	bed	six
mop	cup	jam	bell
lid	box	gum	can

Page 12

Name

Beginning and Ending Sound Review

Say each picture name. Listen to the **first** and **last sound**. Print the letters that stand for the first and last sound. Color the pictures.

h(e)n

bat	hen	pig	dog
bus	cat	web	wig
pot	jug	hat	vet
mix	fox	rug	bag

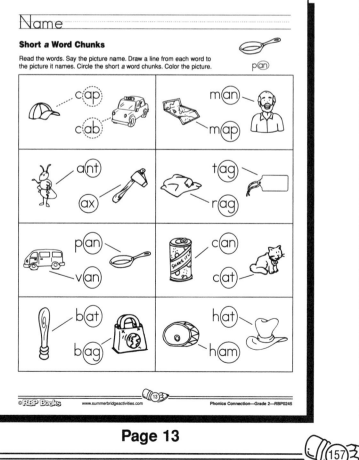

Page 13

Name

Short *a* Word Chunks

Read the words. Say the picture name. Draw a line from each word to the picture it names. Circle the short *a* word chunks. Color the picture.

p(an)

c(ap) / c(ab)   m(an) / m(ap)

a(nt) / (ax)   t(ag) / r(ag)

p(an) / v(an)   c(an) / c(at)

b(at) / b(ag)   h(at) / h(am)

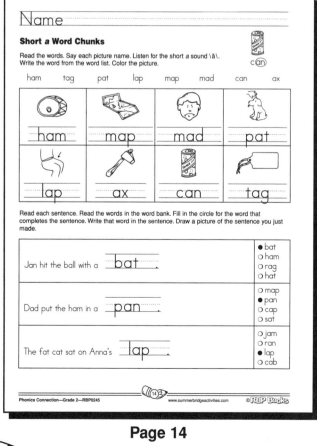

Page 14

Name

Short *a* Word Chunks

Read the words. Say each picture name. Listen for the short *a* sound \ă\. Write the word from the word list. Color the picture.

c(an)

ham   tag   pat   lap   map   mad   can   ax

| ham | map | mad | pat |
| lap | ax | can | tag |

Read each sentence. Read the words in the word bank. Fill in the circle for the word that completes the sentence. Write that word in the sentence. Draw a picture of the sentence you just made.

Jan hit the ball with a	bat.	● bat ○ ham ○ rag ○ hat
Dad put the ham in a	pan.	○ map ● pan ○ cap ○ sat
The fat cat sat on Anna's	lap.	○ jam ○ ran ● lap ○ cab

Answer Pages

Page 15

Name

Short *a* Word Chunks

Read the story below. Say each word. Listen carefully for the short *a* sound \ă\. Draw a line under each word with the short *a* sound. Write your favorites in the short *a* word bank. Add to or color the picture.

r<u>a</u>g

Sam had something.
He hid it under the mat.
Dad said, "It is a cat?"
Sam hid it under the hat.
Jan said, "It is a bat?"
Sam hid it under the rag.
Dan said, "It is a rat?"
Sam took it out.
"AN ALLIGATOR!" said Dad, Jan, and Dan.

Read each question about the story. Fill in the circle by the correct answer. Write the word on the line.

	Short *a* Word Bank
1. Dad said it was a ___cat___ . ○ fat ○ van ○ cap ● cat 2. Jan said it was a ___bat___ . ○ ham ○ sad ○ fan ● bat	Sam Dad Jan etc.

Write an answer.
What did you think it was?
<u>Answers will vary</u> .

On another piece of paper write a story about a time you tricked a friend or a friend tricked you.

Page 15

Page 16

Name

Short *i* Word Chunks

Read the words. Say each picture name. Draw a line from each word to the picture it names. Circle the short *i* word chunks. Color the pictures.

s(ip)

p(ig) w(ig)
s(it) m(itt)
r(ip) z(ip)
b(ib) cr(ib)
s(ip) sh(ip)
m(ix) s(ix)
sp(ill) dr(ill)
dr(ip) d(ig)

Page 16

Page 17

Name

Short *i* Word Chunks

Read the words. Say each picture name. Listen for the short *i* sound \ĭ\. Write the word from the word list. Color the picture.

d(ig)

pin   fix   lid   lips   kit   rib   fin   pit

pin	fin	pit	lips
lid	kit	rib	fix

Read each sentence. Read the words in the word bank. Fill in the circle for the word that completes the sentence. Write that word in the sentence. Draw a picture of the sentence you just made.

The pig liked to ___dig___ in the mud.	○ hit ○ win ● dig ○ did
Is your fish ___big___ or little?	● big ○ sit ○ tin ○ rid
The lid did not fit the ___dish___ .	○ it ○ fix ○ hid ● dish

Page 17

Page 18

Name

Short *i* Word Chunks

Read the story below. Say each word. Listen carefully for the short *i* sound \ĭ\. Draw a line under each word with the short *i* sound. Write your favorites in the short *i* word bank. Add to or color the picture.

m<u>i</u>tt

Once there was a big pink pig
who wore a yellow wig.
He liked to dance an Irish jig.
He danced under the fig tree.
Six purple inchworms hid by a twig
Their eyes fixed on the pig.
The pig tripped on a stick.
The inchworms picked up the pig.
They fixed his hurt lip.

Read each question about the story. Fill in the circle by the correct answer. Write the word on the line.

	Short *i* Word Bank
1. The pig was ___big___ . ○ fat ● big ○ little ○ thin 2. What kind of tree was in the story? ___fig___ ○ apple ○ pear ● fig ○ date	big wig jig etc.

Write an answer.
How many inchworms were there?
<u>There were six inchworms.</u>

On another piece of paper write a story about a pig. What can the pig do? What color is it? How big is it?

Page 18

Answer Pages

Page 19

Name

Short *u* Word Chunks

Read the words. Say the picture names. Draw a line from each word to the picture it names. Circle the short *u* word chunks. Color the pictures.

c(up)

b(ug)
r(ug)

c(ut)
c(ub)

h(ug)
h(ut)

b(us)
b(un)

dr(um)
g(um)

tr(uck)
t(ug)

m(ud)
b(ud)

p(up)
c(up)

Page 19

Page 20

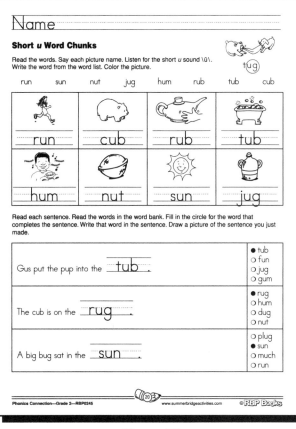

Name

Short *u* Word Chunks

Read the words. Say each picture name. Listen for the short *u* sound \ū\. Write the word from the word list. Color the picture.

tug

run   sun   nut   jug   hum   rub   tub   cub

| run | cub | rub | tub |
| hum | nut | sun | jug |

Read each sentence. Read the words in the word bank. Fill in the circle for the word that completes the sentence. Write that word in the sentence. Draw a picture of the sentence you just made.

Gus put the pup into the _tub_.	● tub ○ fun ○ jug ○ gum
The cub is on the _rug_.	● rug ○ hum ○ dug ○ nut
A big bug sat in the _sun_.	○ plug ● sun ○ much ○ run

Page 20

Page 21

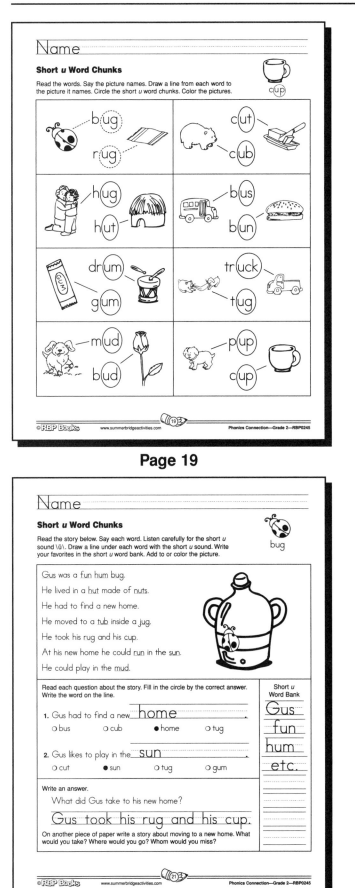

Name

Short *u* Word Chunks

Read the story below. Say each word. Listen carefully for the short *u* sound \ū\. Draw a line under each word with the short *u* sound. Write your favorites in the short *u* word bank. Add to or color the picture.

bug

Gus was a fun hum bug.

He lived in a hut made of nuts.

He had to find a new home.

He moved to a tub inside a jug.

He took his rug and his cup.

At his new home he could run in the sun.

He could play in the mud.

Read each question about the story. Fill in the circle by the correct answer. Write the word on the line.

1. Gus had to find a new _home_
   ○ bus   ○ cub   ● home   ○ tug

2. Gus likes to play in the _sun_
   ○ cut   ● sun   ○ tug   ○ gum

Write an answer.

What did Gus take to his new home?

Gus took his rug and his cup.

On another piece of paper write a story about moving to a new home. What would you take? Where would you go? Whom would you miss?

Short *u* Word Bank

Gus
fun
hum
etc.

Page 21

Page 22

Name

Short *o* Word Chunks

Read the words. Say the picture names. Draw a line from each word to the picture it names. Circle the short *o* word chunks. Color the pictures.

d(og)

d(og)
d(ot)

l(og)
f(og)

p(ot)
p(op)

t(op)
h(op)

p(od)
h(og)

(ox)
f(ox)

c(op)
c(ot)

m(op)
m(om)

Page 22

Page 23

Name

Short *o* Word Chunks

Read the words. Say each picture name. Listen for the short *o* sound \ŏ\. Write the word from the word list. Color the picture.

b(ox)

box   fog   cob   rod   jog   pod   hog   pot

box	jog	pot	cob
hog	pod	fog	rod

Read each sentence. Read the words in the word bank. Fill in the circle for the word that completes the sentence. Write that word in the sentence. Draw a picture of the sentence you just made.

Answers may vary.

My dog likes to sit on the ___log___ .	○ cot ● log ○ box ○ pod
The ___frog___ got hot in the sun.	○ mop ● frog ○ top ○ cob
Mom had to mop up the spill from the ___pot___ .	● pot ○ dog ○ hog ○ lot

Page 23

Page 24

Name

Short *o* Word Chunks

Read the story below. Say each word. Listen carefully for the short *o* sound \ŏ\. Draw a line under each word with the short *o* sound. Write your favorites in the short *o* word bank. Add to or color the picture.

● dot

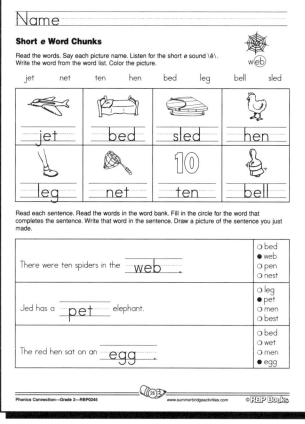

One hot foggy day a frog popped out of his pond.
He wanted to find someone to play with him.
He found his friends ox and octopus.
Octopus could mop floors with his eight legs.
Ox could put the pot on the top cot.
Frog could hop from log to log.
They all had to obey Mom when she said, "Stop."

Read each question about the story. Fill in the circle by the correct answer. Write the word on the line.

1. What kind of day was it? ___foggy___
   ○ hot   ○ cold   ● foggy   ○ warm

2. Who popped out of his pond? ___frog___
   ● frog   ○ dog   ○ ox   ○ octopus

Write an answer.
What could ox do?

___Ox could put the pot on the top cot.___

On another piece of paper write about what you and your friends do at your house or their houses.

Short *o* Word Bank
hot
foggy
frog
etc.

Page 24

Page 25

Name

Short *e* Word Chunks

Read the words. Say the picture names. Draw a line from each word to the picture it names. Circle the short *e* word chunks. Color the pictures.

w(et)

w(eb) / w(et)
sh(ell) / sm(ell)
l(eg) / b(eg)
j(et) / p(et)
st(ep) / sl(ed)
h(en) / m(en)
b(ell) / w(ell)
n(est) / n(et)

Page 25

Page 26

Name

Short *e* Word Chunks

Read the words. Say each picture name. Listen for the short *e* sound \ĕ\. Write the word from the word list. Color the picture.

w(eb)

jet   net   ten   hen   bed   leg   bell   sled

jet	bed	sled	hen
leg	net	ten	bell

Read each sentence. Read the words in the word bank. Fill in the circle for the word that completes the sentence. Write that word in the sentence. Draw a picture of the sentence you just made.

There were ten spiders in the ___web___ .	○ bed ● web ○ pen ○ nest
Jed has a ___pet___ elephant.	○ leg ● pet ○ men ○ best
The red hen sat on an ___egg___ .	○ bed ○ wet ○ men ● egg

Page 26

Answer Pages

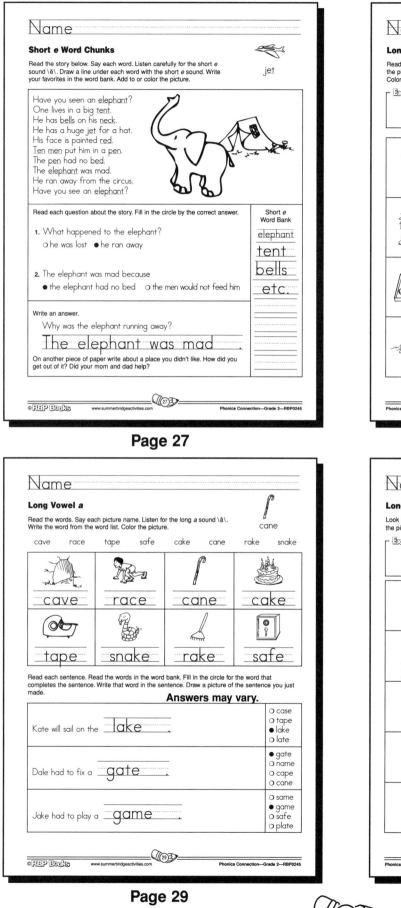

Page 27

Short *e* Word Chunks

Read the story below. Say each word. Listen carefully for the short *e* sound \ĕ\. Draw a line under each word with the short *e* sound. Write your favorites in the word bank. Add to or color the picture.

jet

Have you seen an <u>elephant</u>?
One lives in a big <u>tent</u>.
He has <u>bells</u> on his <u>neck</u>.
He has a huge <u>jet</u> for a hat.
His face is painted <u>red</u>.
<u>Ten</u> <u>men</u> put him in a <u>pen</u>.
The <u>pen</u> had no bed.
The <u>elephant</u> was mad.
He ran away from the circus.
Have you see an <u>elephant</u>?

Read each question about the story. Fill in the circle by the correct answer.

1. What happened to the elephant?
   ○ he was lost   ● he ran away

2. The elephant was mad because
   ● the elephant had no bed   ○ the men would not feed him

Write an answer.
Why was the elephant running away?
The elephant was mad.

On another piece of paper write about a place you didn't like. How did you get out of it? Did your mom and dad help?

Short *e* Word Bank
elephant
tent
bells
etc.

Page 28

Long Vowel *a*

Read the words. Say the picture names. Draw a line from each word to the picture it names. Write the vowel sounds like the example below. Color the pictures.

lake

Example:
căn   cān̄é

Cane has the long *a* sound. This sound is often spelled by ā and silent é.

căn — cān̄é
căp — cāpé
măn — mān̄é
păn — pān̄é
băt — bāké
văn — vāsé
păn — plān̄é
săt — skāté

Page 29

Long Vowel *a*

Read the words. Say each picture name. Listen for the long *a* sound \ā\. Write the word from the word list. Color the picture.

cane

cave   race   tape   safe   cake   cane   rake   snake

cave   race   cane   cake
tape   snake   rake   safe

Read each sentence. Read the words in the word bank. Fill in the circle for the word that completes the sentence. Write that word in the sentence. Draw a picture of the sentence you just made.

Answers may vary.

Kate will sail on the **lake**.
○ case   ○ tape   ● lake   ○ late

Dale had to fix a **gate**.
● gate   ○ name   ○ cape   ○ cane

Jake had to play a **game**.
○ same   ● game   ○ safe   ○ plate

Page 30

Long Vowel *a*

Look at each picture below. Fill in the missing letters in the word below the picture. Listen carefully for the long *a* vowel sound \ā\.

plane

Example:
căn   cān̄é

Cane has the long *a* sound. This sound is often spelled by *a* and silent e.

cane   face   cape
plane   tape   bake
vane   case   mane
cake   snake   pane
vase   lake   lace

www.summerbridgeactivities.com   Phonics Connection—Grade 2—RBP0245

Page 31

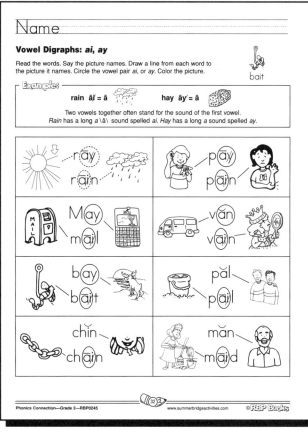

Name

Long Vowel *a*

Read the story below. Say each word. Listen carefully for the long *a* sound \ā\. Draw a line under each word with the long *a* sound. Write your favorites in the long *a* word bank. Add to or color the picture.

rake

There was a drake. His name was Jake.
His best friend was a snake.
His name was Flake.
They liked to go to the lake and eat cake.
One time they met an ape.
He taught them a new game.
They hit a ball and ran to a base.
The game was named baseball.
They had so much fun they went home late.

Read each question about the story. Fill in the circle by the correct answer.

Long *a* Word Bank

1. Who are the characters in the story?
   ● drake and snake   ○ snake and whale

2. Whom did the snake and drake meet?
   ● ape   ○ alligator   ○ whale

Write an answer.
   What new game did they learn to play?

   They learned to play baseball.

On another piece of paper write about your favorite game. Whom do you play it with? What are the rules?

drake
Jake
snake
Flake
etc.

Page 32

Name

Vowel Digraphs: *ai, ay*

Read the words. Say the picture names. Draw a line from each word to the picture it names. Circle the vowel pair *ai*, or *ay*. Color the picture.

bait

Examples:
   rain āĭ = ā   hay āў = ā

Two vowels together often stand for the sound of the first vowel.
Rain has a long *a* \ā\ sound spelled *ai*. *Hay* has a long *a* sound spelled *ay*.

ray / rain
pay / pain
May / mail
van / vain
bay / bait
pal / pail
chin / chain
man / maid

Page 33

Name

Vowel Digraphs: *ai, ay*

Read the words. Say each picture name. Listen for the vowel pair *ai* and *ay* sound. Write the word from the word list. Color the picture.

brain

brain   clay   bait   train   rain   drain   grain   tray

brain	tray	drain	clay
grain	rain	bait	train

Read each sentence. Read the words in the word bank. Fill in the circle for the word that completes the sentence. Write that word in the sentence. Draw a picture of the sentence you just made.

Jane put __bait__ on her hook to catch a fish.
● bait ○ train ○ rain ○ drain

In art class we build with __clay__.
● clay ○ tray ○ ray ○ may

I got a pizza __stain__ on my dress.
● stain ○ chain ○ drain ○ rain

Page 34

Name

Vowel Digraphs: *ai, ay*

Look at each picture below. Fill in the missing letters in the word below the picture. Listen carefully for the vowel pairs *ai* and *ay*.

rain

Examples:
   rain āĭ = ā   hay āў = ā

Two vowels together often stand for the sound of the first vowel.
Rain has a long *a* sound \ā\ spelled *ai*. *Hay* has a long *a* sound spelled *ay*.

safe	rain	lake
ray	rake	May
game	nail	bay
bait	chain	pail
maid	tail	hay

Answer Pages

Page 35

Name

Vowel Digraphs: *ai, ay*

Read the story below. Listen carefully for the vowel pairs *ai* and *ay*. Draw a line under each word with the vowel pair *ai* or *ay*. Write your favorites in the vowel digraph word bank. Add to or color the picture.

ray

A maid named Lorraine lived in Maine.
She went on a train to the beach in May.
She took her dog. He was a Great Dane.
She wanted to fish in the lake.
She put bait on her hook.
Sitting and waiting was a strain.
Then it started to rain.
It was a hurricane!
She got back on the train.
She went home to Maine.

Read each question about the story. Fill in the circle by the correct answer. Write the word on the line.

Vowel Digraph Word Bank

maid
Lorraine
Maine
etc.

1. Lorraine was a ___maid___
   ○ brain   ● maid   ○ ray   ○ chain

2. A Great Dane is a ___dog___
   ○ cat   ● dog   ○ pig   ○ fish

Write an answer.

List the kinds of bait she might use on her hook to catch a fish.

___Answers will vary___

On another piece of paper write a story about a time you went fishing. Did you catch a fish? What bait did you use? How big was the fish?

Page 36

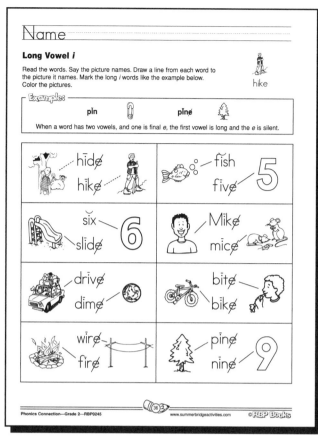

Long Vowel *i*

Read the words. Say the picture names. Draw a line from each word to the picture it names. Mark the long *i* words like the example below. Color the pictures.

hike

Example:
pĭn   pīnĕ

When a word has two vowels, and one is final *e*, the first vowel is long and the *e* is silent.

hīdĕ / hīkĕ	fish / fīvĕ — 5
sĭx — 6 / slīdĕ	Mīkĕ / mīcĕ
drīvĕ / dīmĕ	bītĕ / bīkĕ
wīrĕ / fīrĕ	pīnĕ / nīnĕ — 9

Page 37

Name

Long Vowel *i*

Read the words. Say each picture name. Listen for the long *i* vowel sound. Write the word from the word list. Color the picture.

vine

dive   vine   ride   bride   spider   smile   climb   pipe

dive	smile	pipe	ride
bride	spider	climb	vine

Read each sentence. Read the words in the word bank. Fill in the circle for the word that completes the sentence. Write that word in the sentence. Draw a picture of the sentence you just made.

Sam put a ___tire___ on his car.	○ file ● tire ○ dice ○ fire
We painted our house ___white___.	○ wife ● white ○ wit ○ wide
I like to sit under the ___pine___ trees.	○ pin ○ pipe ● pine ○ pie

Page 38

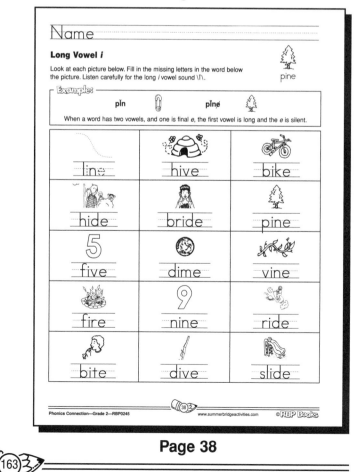

Long Vowel *i*

Look at each picture below. Fill in the missing letters in the word below the picture. Listen carefully for the long *i* vowel sound \ī\.

pine

Example:
pĭn   pīnĕ

When a word has two vowels, and one is final *e*, the first vowel is long and the *e* is silent.

line	hive	bike
hide	bride	pine
five	dime	vine
fire	nine	ride
bite	dive	slide

Answer Pages

Page 39

Long Vowel *i*

Read the story below. Say each word. Listen carefully for the long *i* vowel sound \ī\. Draw a line under each word with the long *i* vowel sound. Write your favorites in the long *i* word bank. Add to or color the picture.

kite

My name is <u>Mike</u>.
Each day I <u>ride</u> my <u>white</u> <u>bike</u>.
I fly my <u>kite</u>.
I eat <u>lime</u> <u>pie</u>.
I <u>climb</u> the <u>pine</u> trees.
I go down the <u>slide</u>.
I catch <u>five</u> fish.
I spend <u>nine</u> <u>dimes</u>.
I play with my <u>nice</u> <u>mice</u>.
I <u>climb</u> into bed at <u>night</u>.
I have a <u>fine</u> <u>life</u>.

Read each question about the story. Fill in the circle by the correct answer. Write the word on the line.

Long *i* Word Bank

Mike
ride
white
etc.

1. Mike had a ___fine___ life.
   ● fine ○ five ○ nine ○ line

2. He likes to ride his ___white___ bike.
   ● white ○ kite ○ slide ○ wide

Write an answer.
What kind of trees did Mike like to climb?

___Mike liked to climb pine trees.___

On another piece of paper make a list of what you do each day.

Page 40

Long Vowel *u*

Read the words. Say the picture names. Draw a line from each word to the picture it names. Mark the sounds of the words like the example below. Color the picture.

cute

Examples:
When a word had two vowels, and one is final *e*, the first vowel is long and the *e* is silent.

cūb¢

When two vowels are together, the first vowel is usually long and the second is silent.

glū¢

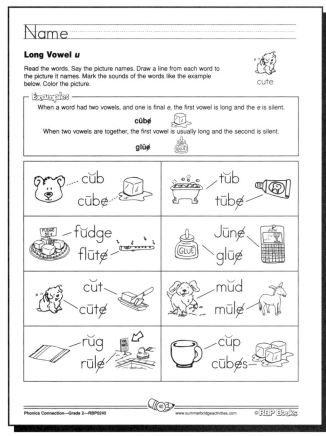

cŭb / cūb¢   tŭb / tūb¢
fŭdge / flūt¢   Jūn¢ / glū¢
cŭt / cūt¢   mŭd / mūl¢
rŭg / rūl¢   cŭp / cūb¢s

Page 41

Long Vowel *u*

Read the words. Say each picture name. Listen for the long *u* vowel sound \ū\. Write the word from the word list. Color the picture.

mule

glue   fuse   bugle   chute   juice   tune   fuel   fruit

| glue | fuel | fuse | chute |
| juice | fruit | tune | bugle |

Read each sentence. Read the words in the word bank. Fill in the circle for the word that completes the sentence. Write that word in the sentence. Draw a picture of the sentence you just made.

Luke can use the ___glue___ to fix his picture.
● glue ○ flag ○ frog ○ fat

Ruth had a ___cute___ kitten.
● cute ○ cut ○ cub ○ cup

Sue can hum a ___tune___.
● tune ○ tub ○ June ○ tot

Page 42

Long Vowel *u*

Look at each picture below. Fill in the missing letters in the word below the picture. Listen carefully for the long *u* sound \ū\.

cube

Examples:
When a word had two vowels, and one is final *e*, the first vowel is long and the *e* is silent.

cūb¢

When two vowels are together, the first vowel is usually long and the second is silent.

glū¢

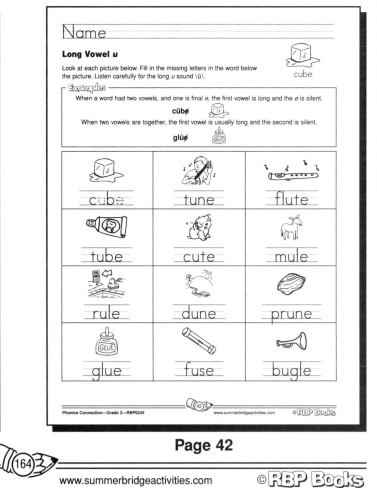

cube	tune	flute
tube	cute	mule
rule	dune	prune
glue	fuse	bugle

Answer Pages

Page 43

Long Vowel *u*

Read the story below. Say each word. Listen carefully for the long *u* vowel sound \ū\. Draw a line under each word with the long *u* vowel sound. Write your favorites in the long *u* word bank. Add to or color the picture.

glue

Sue was a spy.
She was due to find a clue.
She rode her mule to the dunes.
She took water with her.
That was the rule.
She played a tune on the flute as she rode on the mule.
In the dunes she found a tube of blue paint.
The paint tube had fingerprints on it.
That was the clue she needed.

Read each question about the story. Fill in the circle by the correct answer. Write the word on the line.

1. Sue was a __spy__
   ● spy   ○ pie   ○ camel   ○ pup

2. She rode a __mule__
   ○ bike   ● mule   ○ horse   ○ camel

Write an answer.
What was the clue Sue was looking for?
__She was looking for fingerprints.__

On another piece of paper write the story again. This time help Sue find a different clue.

Long *u* Word Bank
Sue
due
clue
etc.

© RBP Books   www.summerbridgeactivities.com   Phonics Connection—Grade 2—RBP0245

Page 43

Page 44

Long Vowel *o*

Read the words. Say the picture names. Draw a line from each word to the picture it names. Mark the vowel sounds like the example below. Color the picture.

nose

Examples:
When a word has two vowels, and one is final *e*, the first vowel is long and the *e* is silent.
rōsé
When two vowels are together, the first vowel is usually long and the second is silent.
tōȧd   tōé

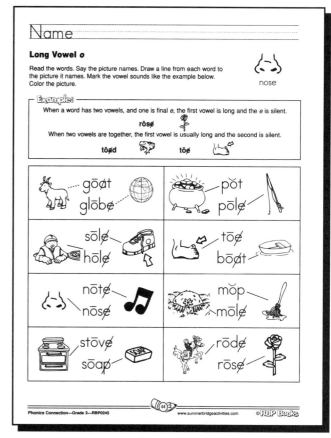

gōȧt / glōbé
pȯt / pōlé
sōlé / hōlé
tōé / bōȧt
nōté / nōsé
mȯp / mōlé
stōvé / sōȧp
rōdé / rōsé

Phonics Connection—Grade 2—RBP0245   www.summerbridgeactivities.com   © RBP Books

Page 44

Page 45

Long Vowel *o*

Read the words. Say each picture name. Listen for the long *o* vowel sound \ō\. Write the word from the word list. Color the picture.

rose

toe   stone   hoe   nose   coat   robe   soap   wrote

toe	soap	coat	wrote
stone	hoe	robe	nose

Read each sentence. Read the words in the word bank. Fill in the circle for the word that completes the sentence. Write that word in the sentence. Draw a picture of the sentence you just made.

A toad is in the __road__.	○ rod ● road ○ rag ○ robe
A mole is in the __hole__.	○ hat ● hole ○ hot ○ hoe
You can smell the rose with your __nose__.	○ not ● nose ○ note ○ hose

© RBP Books   www.summerbridgeactivities.com   Phonics Connection—Grade 2—RBP0245

Page 45

Page 46

Long Vowel *o*

Look at each picture below. Fill in the missing letters in the word below the picture. Listen carefully for the long *o* vowel sound \ō\.

toad

Examples:
When a word has two vowels, and one is final *e*, the first vowel is long and the *e* is silent.
rōsé
When two vowels are together, the first vowel is usually long and the second is silent.
tōȧd   tōé

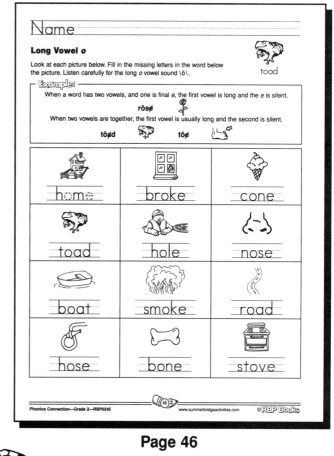

home	broke	cone
toad	hole	nose
boat	smoke	road
hose	bone	stove

Phonics Connection—Grade 2—RBP0245   www.summerbridgeactivities.com   © RBP Books

Page 46

Answer Pages

Page 47

Name

Long Vowel _o_

Read the story below. Say each word. Listen carefully for the long _o_ vowel sound \ō\. Draw a line under each word with the long _o_ vowel sound. Write your favorites in the Long _o_ word bank. Add to or color the picture.

toe

Joan and her goat went for a ride.
They went for a ride in a boat.
They floated on the moat.
A toad jumped into the boat.
He wanted to tell them a joke.
The toad's joke was funny.
Joan broke out laughing,
but the goat groaned.
As quickly as the toad hopped
in he hopped out again.

Knock, Knock...

Read each question about the story. Fill in the circle by the correct answer. Write the word on the line.

Long _o_ Word Bank

Joan
goat
boat
etc.

1. Joan went in a boat with a _goat_
   ○ coat ● goat ○ gold ○ goal

2. The toad told a _joke_
   ○ story ● joke ○ poem ○ song

Write an answer.
How would you feel if someone hopped in your boat?
Answers will vary

On another piece of paper write the funniest joke you have ever heard.

© RBP Books www.summerbridgeactivities.com 47 Phonics Connection—Grade 2—RBP0245

Page 47

Page 48

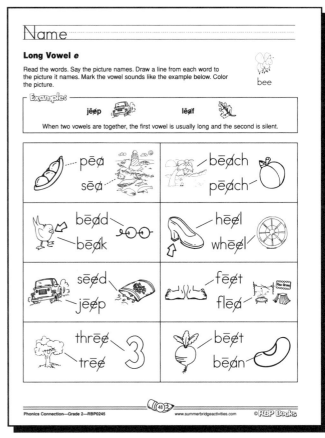

Page 48

Page 49

Name

Long Vowel _e_

Read the words. Say each picture name. Listen for the long _e_ vowel sound \ē\. Write the word from the word list. Color the picture.

pea

seal   seat   leaf   heat   sheep   bee   peek   knee

seal	heat	peek	sheep
bee	seat	knee	leaf

Read each sentence. Read the words in the word bank. Fill in the circle for the word that completes the sentence. Write that word in the sentence. Draw a picture of the sentence you just made.

Do you like roast _beef_ ?	● beef ○ wheat ○ peach ○ leaf
The farmer had nine _sheep_ .	○ ships ● sheep ○ seat ○ shape
The children were eating _meatballs_ .	○ heat ○ knees ● meatballs ○ bees

© RBP Books www.summerbridgeactivities.com 49 Phonics Connection—Grade 2—RBP0245

Page 49

Page 50

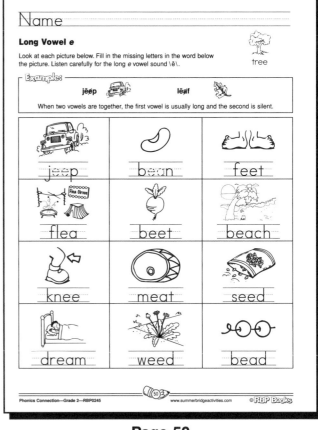

Page 50

Answer Pages

Page 51

Name

Long Vowel e

Read the story below. Say each word. Listen carefully for the long e vowel sound \ē\. Draw a line under each word with the long e vowel sound. Write your favorites in the long e word bank. Add to or color the picture.

wheel

Flea went to Sheep's house to eat a meal.
Sheep brought Flea some peas.
Flea said, "I do not want peas."
So, Sheep brought him beets.
Flea said, " I do not want beets."
So Sheep brought him weeds.
"Weeds?" screeched Flea. "I want something sweet."
So Sheep brought him nothing more.
Sheep sat down to eat peaches and cream.

Read each question about the story. Fill in the circle by the correct answer. Write the word on the line.

Long e Word Bank

flea
sheep
eat
etc.

1. Do you think Flea was __nice__?
   ● nice ○ tired ○ mean ○ angry

2. What did Flea want? __something sweet.__
   ○ beets ○ peas ○ pie ● something sweet

Write an answer.
What would you have done if you were the sheep?
__Answers will vary__

On another piece of paper write about a time you had to eat something you didn't like or want. How did it make you feel?

Page 51

Page 52

Name

Sounds of y

Read the words. Say the picture names. Draw a line from each word to the picture it names. Write in whether the y sounds like y, i, or e. Follow the example. Color the picture.

story

Examples:
The letter y has a sound of \y\, as in yak. The letter y at the end of some words can stand for the long i sound \ī\ as in fly. The letter y at the end of some words can also stand for the long e sound \ē\ as in story.

yak   fly = flī   story = storē

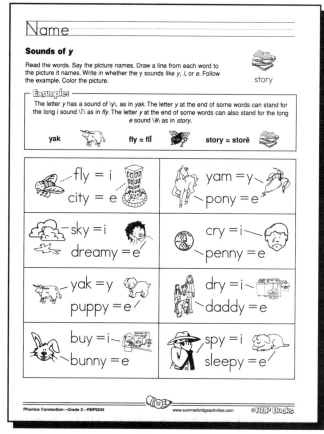

fly = i
city = e

yam = y
pony = e

sky = i
dreamy = e

cry = i
penny = e

yak = y
puppy = e

dry = i
daddy = e

buy = i
bunny = e

spy = i
sleepy = e

Page 52

Page 53

Name

Sounds of y

Read the words. Say each picture name. Listen for the sound of y. Write the word from the word list. Color the picture.

candy

candy   daddy   fly   bunny   cry   muddy   party   fifty

candy   fifty   party   bunny

daddy   cry   muddy   fly

Read each sentence. Read the words in the word bank. Fill in the circle for the word that completes the sentence. Write that word in the sentence. Draw a picture of the sentence you just made.

Our boots were __muddy__.
○ fifty ● muddy ○ bunny ○ fly

We went to the store to get a __yo-yo__.
○ penny ● yo-yo ○ party ○ cry

Did you see the eagle in the __sky__?
○ pie ○ sly ● sky ○ fry

Page 53

Page 54

Name

Sounds of y

Look at each picture below. Fill in the missing letters in the word below the picture. Listen carefully for all the different y sounds.

baby

Examples:
yam = y   fly = ī   puppy = ē

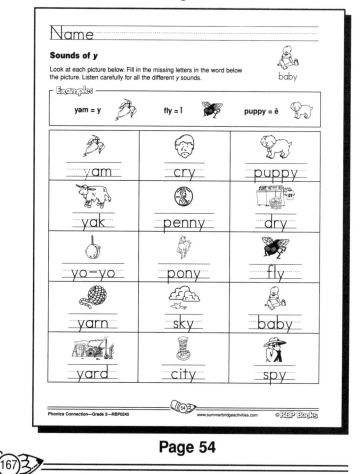

yam   cry   puppy

yak   penny   dry

yo-yo   pony   fly

yarn   sky   baby

yard   city   spy

Page 54

Answer Pages

Page 55

Name

Sounds of y

Read the story below. Say each word. Listen carefully for the sound of *y*. Draw a line under each word with the sound of *y*. Write your favorites in the *y* word bank. Add to or color the picture.

fly

Ziggy the pink piggy was very shy.
She was having a birthday party.
She invited Benny the white bunny.
She invited Teddy the blue fly.
Benny gave her a yellow daisy.
Teddy gave her sticky green candy.
They all ate a big cream pie.
Benny the white bunny said, "Good-bye."
Then Teddy the blue fly said, "Good-bye."

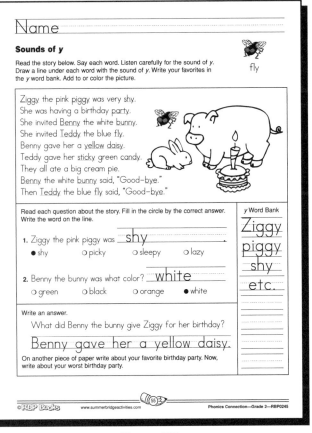

Read each question about the story. Fill in the circle by the correct answer. Write the word on the line.

y Word Bank
Ziggy
piggy
shy
etc.

1. Ziggy the pink piggy was __shy__
   ● shy   ○ picky   ○ sleepy   ○ lazy

2. Benny the bunny was what color? __white__
   ○ green   ○ black   ○ orange   ● white

Write an answer.
What did Benny the bunny give Ziggy for her birthday?
__Benny gave her a yellow daisy.__

On another piece of paper write about your favorite birthday party. Now, write about your worst birthday party.

Page 55

Page 56

Name

Hard and Soft c

Read the words. Say the picture names. Draw a line from each word to the picture it names. In the square write the *c* sound for that picture. Color the picture.

Examples:
The letter *c* followed by *e, i,* or *y* usually stands for the soft *c*, as in *mice.*
The letter *c* followed by any other letter usually stands for the hard sound of *c*, as in *cat.*

mice = s   cat = k

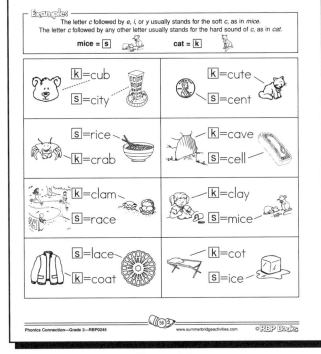

k=cub / s=city	k=cute / s=cent
s=rice / k=crab	k=cave / s=cell
k=clam / s=race	k=clay / s=mice
s=lace / k=coat	k=cot / s=ice

Page 56

Page 57

Name

Hard and Soft c

Read the words. Say each picture name. Listen for the hard and soft *c*. Write the word from the word list. Color the picture.

cap   lace   calf   face   fence   cube   circus   cane

cap	circus	face	ice
calf	cane	lace	fence

Read each sentence. Fill in the circle for the word that makes the same sound as the underlined word. Draw a picture of the sentence you just made.

The letter *c* followed by *e, i,* or *y* usually stands for the soft *c*, as in *mice.* The letter *c* followed by any other letter usually stands for the hard sound of *c*, as in *cat.*

The crab lives on the beach.	● k ○ s
The mice chased the cat.	○ k ● s
A camel called home on his cell phone.	○ k ● s

Page 57

Page 58

Name

Hard and Soft g

Read the words. Say the picture names. Draw a line from each word to the picture it names. In the box write the sound of the hard *g* with the letter *g* or soft *g* with the letter *j*. Color the picture.

Examples:
The letter *g* followed by *e, i,* or *y* often stands for the soft sound of *g*, as in *giraffe.* The letter *g* followed by any other letter usually stands for the hard sound of *g*, as in *goat.*

ge, gi, gy = j   giraffe = j   gu, go, ga = g   goat = g

g=gate / j=gym	j=cage / g=gold
g=gas / g=gull	j=giant / g=game
j=page / g=goat	g=dog / j=magic
j=gem / g=flag	g=frog / j=orange

Page 58

Answer Pages

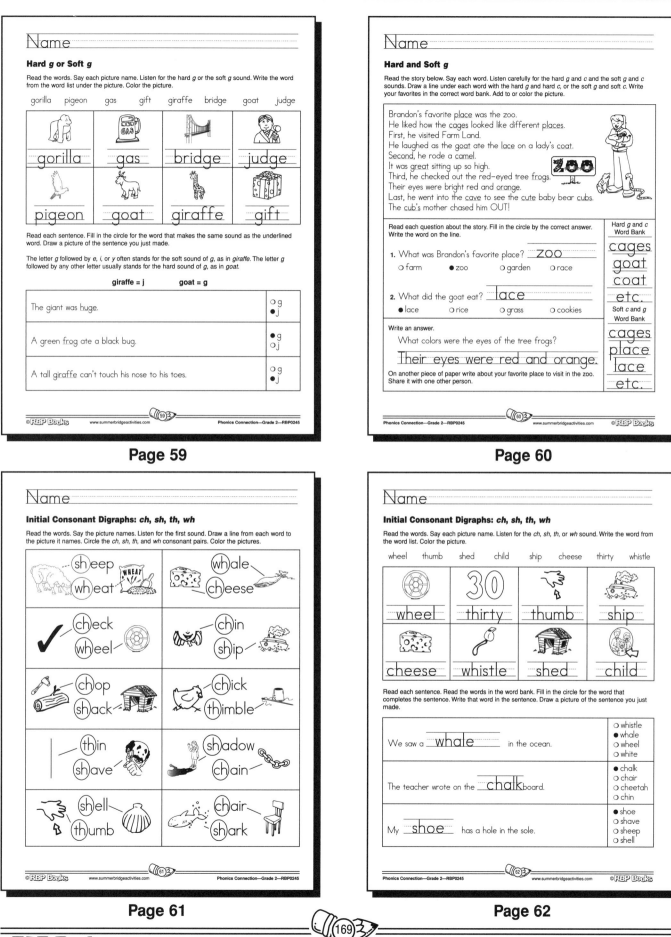

Page 59

Name

Hard g or Soft g

Read the words. Say each picture name. Listen for the hard g or the soft g sound. Write the word from the word list under the picture. Color the picture.

gorilla   pigeon   gas   gift   giraffe   bridge   goat   judge

gorilla	gas	bridge	judge
pigeon	goat	giraffe	gift

Read each sentence. Fill in the circle for the word that makes the same sound as the underlined word. Draw a picture of the sentence you just made.

The letter g followed by e, i, or y often stands for the soft sound of g, as in *giraffe*. The letter g followed by any other letter usually stands for the hard sound of g, as in *goat*.

giraffe = j   goat = g

The giant was huge.	○ g ● j
A green frog ate a black bug.	● g ○ j
A tall giraffe can't touch his nose to his toes.	○ g ● j

Page 60

Name

Hard and Soft g

Read the story below. Say each word. Listen carefully for the hard g and c and the soft g and c sounds. Draw a line under each word with the hard g and hard c, or the soft g and soft c. Write your favorites in the correct word bank. Add to or color the picture.

Brandon's favorite place was the zoo.
He liked how the cages looked like different places.
First, he visited Farm Land.
He laughed as the goat ate the lace on a lady's coat.
Second, he rode a camel.
It was great sitting up so high.
Third, he checked out the red-eyed tree frogs.
Their eyes were bright red and orange.
Last, he went into the cave to see the cute baby bear cubs.
The cub's mother chased him OUT!

Read each question about the story. Fill in the circle by the correct answer. Write the word on the line.

1. What was Brandon's favorite place? **zoo**
   ○ farm   ● zoo   ○ garden   ○ race

2. What did the goat eat? **lace**
   ● lace   ○ rice   ○ grass   ○ cookies

Write an answer.
   What colors were the eyes of the tree frogs?
   Their eyes were red and orange.
On another piece of paper write about your favorite place to visit in the zoo. Share it with one other person.

Hard g and c Word Bank
cages
goat
coat
etc.

Soft c and g Word Bank
cages
place
lace
etc.

Page 61

Name

Initial Consonant Digraphs: ch, sh, th, wh

Read the words. Say the picture names. Listen for the first sound. Draw a line from each word to the picture it names. Circle the ch, sh, th, and wh consonant pairs. Color the pictures.

sheep / wheat	whale / cheese
✔ check / wheel	chin / ship
chop / shack	chick / thimble
thin / shave	shadow / chain
shell / thumb	chair / shark

Page 62

Name

Initial Consonant Digraphs: ch, sh, th, wh

Read the words. Say each picture name. Listen for the ch, sh, th, or wh sound. Write the word from the word list. Color the picture.

wheel   thumb   shed   child   ship   cheese   thirty   whistle

wheel	thirty	thumb	ship
cheese	whistle	shed	child

Read each sentence. Read the words in the word bank. Fill in the circle for the word that completes the sentence. Write that word in the sentence. Draw a picture of the sentence you just made.

We saw a **whale** in the ocean.	○ whistle ● whale ○ wheel ○ white
The teacher wrote on the **chalk**board.	● chalk ○ chair ○ cheetah ○ chin
My **shoe** has a hole in the sole.	● shoe ○ shave ○ sheep ○ shell

Answer Pages

Page 63

Name

Initial Consonant Digraphs: *ch, sh, th, wh*

Look at each picture below. Fill in the missing letters in the word below the picture. Listen carefully for the *ch, sh, th,* or *wh* sound.

Examples:
(ch)eese   (sh)eep   (th)umb   (wh)ale

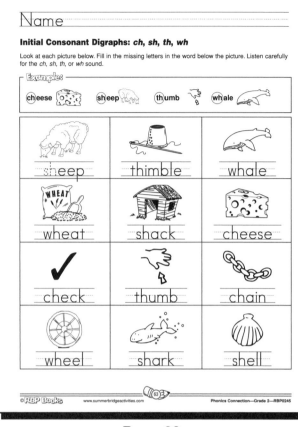

sheep   thimble   whale

wheat   shack   cheese

check   thumb   chain

wheel   shark   shell

Page 64

Name

Initial Consonant Digraphs: *ch, sh, th, wh*

Read the story below. Say each word. Listen carefully for the consonant pairs *ch, sh, th,* and *wh.* Draw a line under each word with the consonant pairs *ch, sh, th,* or *wh.* Write your favorites in the word bank. Add to or color the picture.

In the ocean there was a big commotion.
The shark said, "I am the champion."
The whale said, "No, I am the champion."
So, they had a race.
The whistle blew, and a great whoop
went up from all the animals.
Off went the shark and the whale.
They swam down to the shrimp,
around the giant seashell, and
the race ended at the ship.
The judges were the cheetah, chick, and sheep.
They waited on the ship for the winner.

I am the champion.

No, I am the champion.

Read each question about the story. Fill in the circle by the correct answer. Write the word on the line.

1. Who was one of the judges?   **cheetah**
   ○ shark   ○ whale   ○ shrimp   ● cheetah

2. What sound started the race?   **whistle**
   ● whistle   ○ pistol   ○ thistle   ○ whoop

Write an answer.
Where were the shark and the whale swimming to?

They were swimming to the ship.

On another piece of paper write what happens at the end of the race. Who wins the race?

Digraph Word Bank

shark
there
whale
etc.

Page 65

Name

Final Consonant Digraphs and Trigraphs: *ch, ck, gh, ng, nk, sh, th, tch*

Read the words. Say the picture names. Draw a line from each word to the picture it names. Circle the consonant group: *ch, ck, gh, ng, nk, sh, th, tch.* Color the picture.

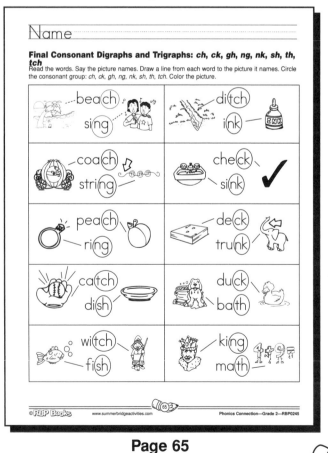

bea(ch)   si(ng)
di(tch)   i(nk)
coa(ch)   stri(ng)
che(ck)   si(nk)
pea(ch)   ri(ng)
de(ck)   tru(nk)
ca(tch)   di(sh)
du(ck)   ba(th)
wi(tch)   fi(sh)
ki(ng)   ma(th)

Page 66

Name

Final Consonant Digraphs and Trigraphs: *ch, ck, gh, ng, nk, sh, th, tch*

Read the words. Say each picture name. Listen for the consonant group: *ch, ck, gh, ng, nk, sh, th, tch.* Write the word from the word list. Color the picture.

pouch   tooth   fetch   patch   back   slick   ring   trash

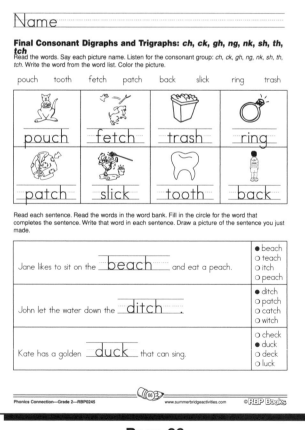

pouch   fetch   trash   ring

patch   slick   tooth   back

Read each sentence. Read the words in the word bank. Fill in the circle for the word that completes the sentence. Write that word in each sentence. Draw a picture of the sentence you just made.

Jane likes to sit on the **beach** and eat a peach.
● beach   ○ teach   ○ itch   ○ peach

John let the water down the **ditch**.
● ditch   ○ patch   ○ catch   ○ witch

Kate has a golden **duck** that can sing.
○ check   ● duck   ○ deck   ○ luck

Answer Pages

Page 67

Final Consonant Digraphs and Trigraphs: *ch, ck, gh, ng, nk, sh, th, tch*
Look at each picture below. Fill in the missing letters in the word below the picture. Listen for the consonant groups: *ch, ck, gh, ng, nk, sh, th, tch*.

beach	sing	coach
string	peach	ring
bath	dish	witch
fish	ditch	sink

Page 67

Page 68

Final Consonant Digraphs
Read the story below. Say each word. Listen for the consonant pairs: *ch, ck, gh, ng, nk, sh, th, tch*. Draw a line under each word with consonant pairs. Write your favorites in the digraph word bank. Add to or color the picture.

The King had a very busy day.
He made a list of things to do:
put on my ring,
take a long bath,
walk on the beach,
eat a peach,
see Grouchy Duck,
drink spring water,
have a dish of fish,
put my feet in the ditch,
go see the witch,
clean out the barn.

Read each question about the story. Fill in the circle by the correct answer.

1. What did the king put on?
   ● ring   ○ thing   ○ speech   ○ bath

2. What did he eat in a dish?
   ○ camel   ● fish   ○ peach   ○ song

Write an answer.
Why do you think he wanted to walk on the beach?
Answers will vary

On another piece of paper make a list of things you do every day. What is your school schedule?

Digraph Word Bank
King
ring
bath
etc.

Page 68

Page 69

Initial *s* Clusters: *sc, sk, sn, sp, st, sm, sw, sq*

Read the words. Say the picture names. Draw a line from each word to the picture it names. Circle the initial *s* cluster in each word. Color the picture.

scale, smog
skeleton, square
scarf, stick
skirt, snake
snail, stem
spider, smoke
squid, scorpion
spot, ski
swim, scout
smile, skate

Page 69

Page 70

Initial *s* Clusters: *sc, sq, sh, sp, st, sm, sk, sw*

Read the words. Say each picture name. Listen for the initial *s* cluster. Write the word from the word list. Color the picture.

scone   squirrel   shop   spoon   stage   smoke   skunk   swing

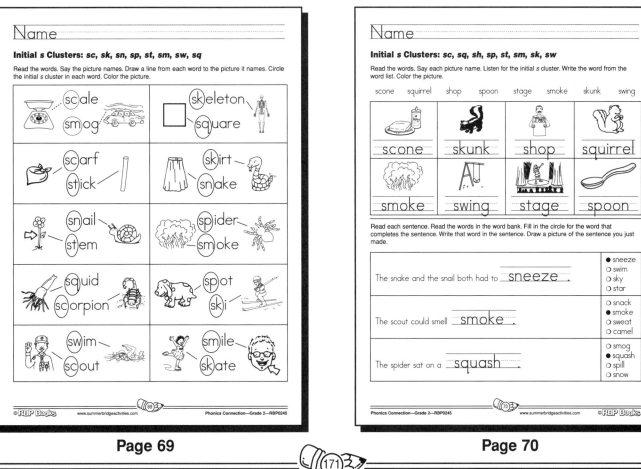

| scone | skunk | shop | squirrel |
| smoke | swing | stage | spoon |

Read each sentence. Read the words in the word bank. Fill in the circle for the word that completes the sentence. Write that word in the sentence. Draw a picture of the sentence you just made.

The snake and the snail both had to _sneeze_.	● sneeze ○ swim ○ sky ○ star
The scout could smell _smoke_.	○ snack ● smoke ○ sweat ○ camel
The spider sat on a _squash_.	○ smog ● squash ○ spill ○ snow

Page 70

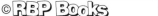

Answer Pages

Page 71

Name

Initial s Clusters: sc, sn, sp, st, sm, sw, sq

Look at each picture below. Fill in the missing letters in the word below the picture. Listen carefully for the s cluster sound.

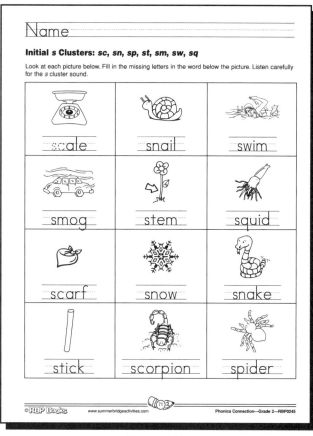

scale	snail	swim
smog	stem	squid
scarf	snow	snake
stick	scorpion	spider

Page 72

Name

Initial s Clusters: sc, sk, sc, sk, sn, sp, st, sm, sw, sq

Read the story below. Say each word. Listen carefully for the s cluster sound. Draw a line under each word with the sound. Write your favorites in the word bank. Add to or color the picture.

A squid has eight arms. He lives in the ocean.
When he feels he is in danger,
he swims away. He also sprays ink.
He can swim very swiftly.
Squid move around in schools.
They eat snails, shrimp, crabs, and lobster.
Squid have no skeletons.
Humans can see squid when
they go diving in the ocean.
Squid can change color to help them hide.

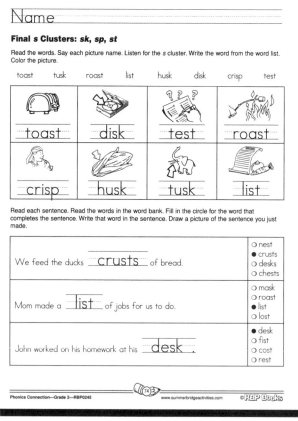

Read each question about the story. Fill in the circle by the correct answer.

1. How many arms do squid have?
   ○ two   ○ four   ○ six   ● eight

2. What do squid eat?
   ○ camel   ○ people   ● shrimp   ○ ships

s Cluster Word Bank
squid
swims
sprays
etc.

Write an answer.
Would you like to go diving in the ocean?
Answers will vary.

On another paper write how you would feel if you saw a squid in the ocean. How would you like swimming at the bottom of the ocean?

Page 73

Name

Final s Clusters: sk, sp, st

Read the words. Say the picture names. Draw a line from each word to the picture it names. Circle the s cluster in each word. Color the picture.

co(st) / de(sk)	te(st) / ca(st)
du(st) / gra(sp)	du(sk) / fi(st)
ne(st) / re(st)	ma(sk) / mi(st)
che(st) / cri(sp)	wa(sp) / ve(st)
toa(st) / hu(sk)	te(st) / di(sk)

Page 74

Name

Final s Clusters: sk, sp, st

Read the words. Say each picture name. Listen for the s cluster. Write the word from the word list. Color the picture.

toast   tusk   roast   list   husk   disk   crisp   test

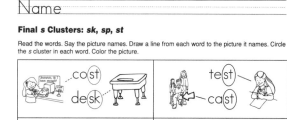

| toast | disk | test | roast |
| crisp | husk | tusk | list |

Read each sentence. Read the words in the word bank. Fill in the circle for the word that completes the sentence. Write that word in the sentence. Draw a picture of the sentence you just made.

We feed the ducks __crusts__ of bread.	○ nest ● crusts ○ desks ○ chests
Mom made a __list__ of jobs for us to do.	○ mask ○ roast ● list ○ lost
John worked on his homework at his __desk__.	● desk ○ fist ○ cost ○ rest

Answer Pages

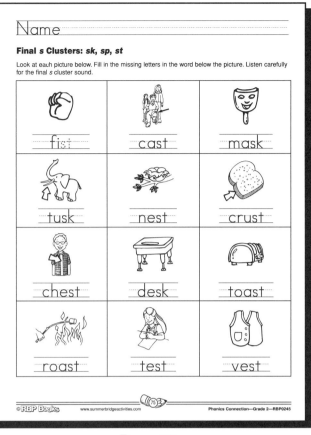

Page 75

Page 76

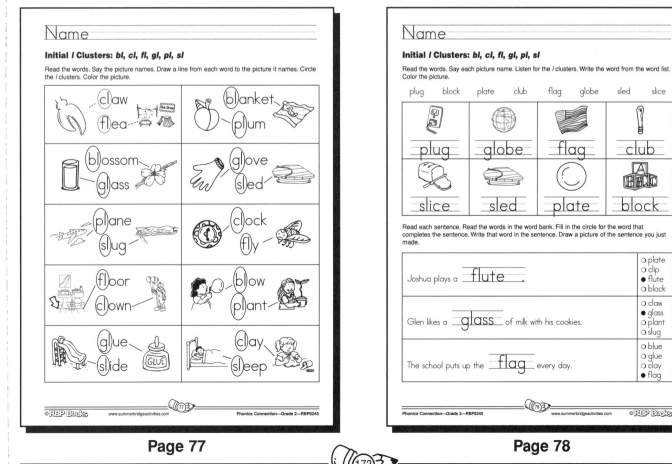

Page 77

Page 78

© RBP Books www.summerbridgeactivities.com   Phonics Connection—Grade 2—RBP0245

Answer Pages

Page 79

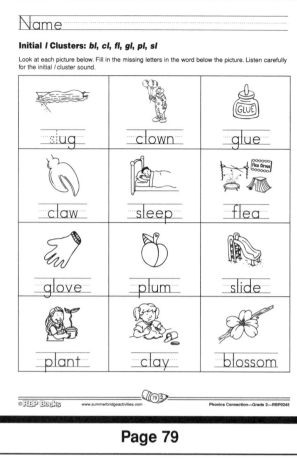

Name

Initial l Clusters: bl, cl, fl, gl, pl, sl

Look at each picture below. Fill in the missing letters in the word below the picture. Listen carefully for the initial l cluster sound.

slug	clown	glue
claw	sleep	flea
glove	plum	slide
plant	clay	blossom

Page 80

Name

Initial l Clusters: bl, cl, fl, gl, pl, sl

Read the story below. Say each word. Listen carefully for the initial l cluster. Draw a line under each word with an l cluster. Write your favorites in the word bank. Add to or color the picture.

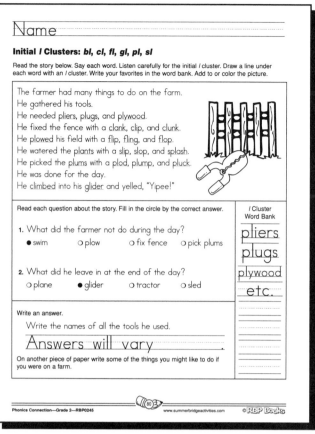

The farmer had many things to do on the farm.
He gathered his tools.
He needed pliers, plugs, and plywood.
He fixed the fence with a clank, clip, and clunk.
He plowed his field with a flip, fling, and flop.
He watered the plants with a slip, slop, and splash.
He picked the plums with a plod, plump, and pluck.
He was done for the day.
He climbed into his glider and yelled, "Yipee!"

Read each question about the story. Fill in the circle by the correct answer.

1. What did the farmer not do during the day?
   ● swim   ○ plow   ○ fix fence   ○ pick plums

2. What did he leave in at the end of the day?
   ○ plane   ● glider   ○ tractor   ○ sled

Write an answer.
   Write the names of all the tools he used.
   Answers will vary

On another piece of paper write some of the things you might like to do if you were on a farm.

l Cluster Word Bank
pliers
plugs
plywood
etc.

Page 81

Name

Initial r Clusters: br, fr, tr, cr, gr, dr, wr, pr

Read the words. Say the picture names. Draw a line from each word to the picture it names. Circle the r cluster. Color the pictures.

brush / frog	freckle / train
trash / crib	crayon / grass
grape / wrench	drain / crab
dress / prince	brain / trap
prize / branch	drum / grin

Page 82

Name

Initial r Clusters: br, fr, tr, cr, gr, dr, wr, pr

Read the words. Say each picture name. Listen for the r clusters. Write the word from the word list. Color the picture.

frame   crow   tray   bride   grass   crib   wrist   drive

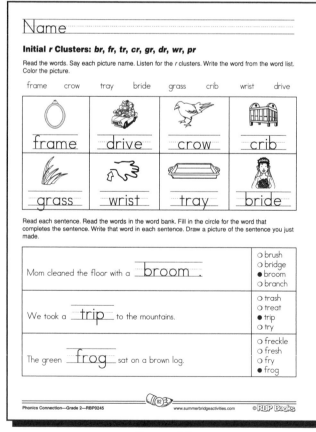

frame	drive	crow	crib
grass	wrist	tray	bride

Read each sentence. Read the words in the word bank. Fill in the circle for the word that completes the sentence. Write that word in each sentence. Draw a picture of the sentence you just made.

Mom cleaned the floor with a __broom__.	○ brush ○ bridge ● broom ○ branch
We took a __trip__ to the mountains.	○ trash ○ treat ● trip ○ try
The green __frog__ sat on a brown log.	○ freckle ○ fresh ○ fry ● frog

Answer Pages

Page 83

Page 84

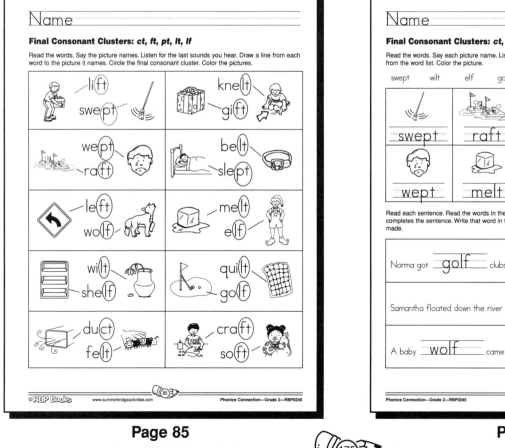

Page 85

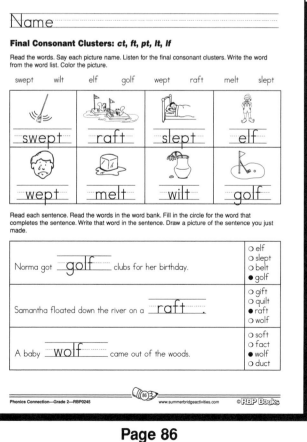

Page 86

www.summerbridgeactivities.com Phonics Connection—Grade 2—RBP0245

Answer Pages

Page 87

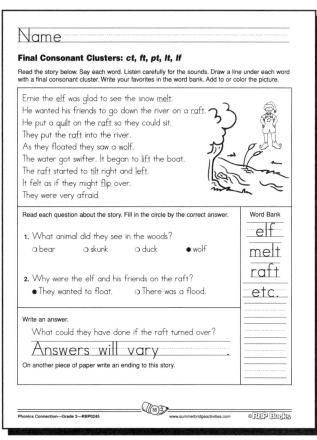

Page 88

Page 89

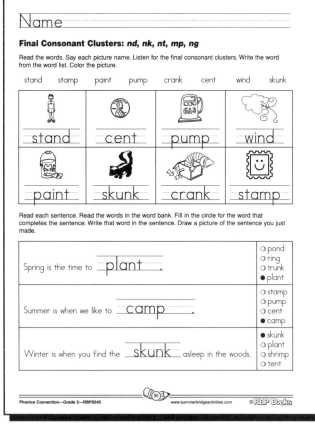

Page 90

Answer Pages

Page 91

Name

Final Consonant Clusters: *nd, nk, nt, mp, ng*

Look at each picture below. Listen carefully for the final consonant cluster. Fill in the missing letters in the word below the picture.

wind | ant | ring
tent | lamp | pond
jump | hand | plant
camp | crank | sang

Page 92

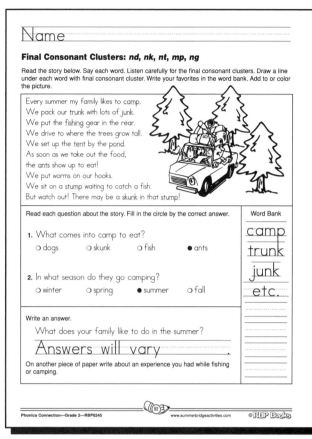

Name

Final Consonant Clusters: *nd, nk, nt, mp, ng*

Read the story below. Say each word. Listen carefully for the final consonant clusters. Draw a line under each word with final consonant cluster. Write your favorites in the word bank. Add to or color the picture.

Every summer my family likes to camp.
We pack our trunk with lots of junk.
We put the fishing gear in the rear.
We drive to where the trees grow tall.
We set up the tent by the pond.
As soon as we take out the food,
the ants show up to eat!
We put worms on our hooks.
We sit on a stump waiting to catch a fish.
But watch out! There may be a skunk in that stump!

Read each question about the story. Fill in the circle by the correct answer.

1. What comes into camp to eat?
   ○ dogs   ○ skunk   ○ fish   ● ants

2. In what season do they go camping?
   ○ winter   ○ spring   ● summer   ○ fall

Write an answer.
   What does your family like to do in the summer?
   Answers will vary.

On another piece of paper write about an experience you had while fishing or camping.

Word Bank
camp
trunk
junk
etc.

Page 93

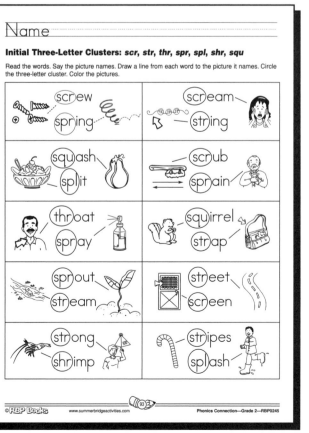

Name

Initial Three-Letter Clusters: *scr, str, thr, spr, spl, shr, squ*

Read the words. Say the picture names. Draw a line from each word to the picture it names. Circle the three-letter cluster. Color the pictures.

screw / spring | scream / string
squash / split | scrub / sprain
throat / spray | squirrel / strap
sprout / stream | street / screen
strong / shrimp | stripes / splash

Page 94

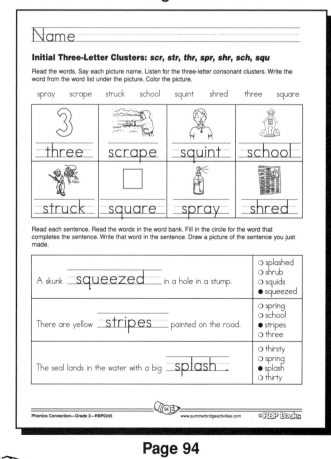

Name

Initial Three-Letter Clusters: *scr, str, thr, spr, shr, sch, squ*

Read the words. Say each picture name. Listen for the three-letter consonant clusters. Write the word from the word list under the picture. Color the picture.

spray   scrape   struck   school   squint   shred   three   square

three | scrape | squint | school
struck | square | spray | shred

Read each sentence. Read the words in the word bank. Fill in the circle for the word that completes the sentence. Write that word in the sentence. Draw a picture of the sentence you just made.

A skunk __squeezed__ in a hole in a stump.
   ○ splashed
   ○ shrub
   ○ squids
   ● squeezed

There are yellow __stripes__ painted on the road.
   ○ spring
   ○ school
   ● stripes
   ○ three

The seal lands in the water with a big __splash__.
   ○ thirsty
   ○ spring
   ● splash
   ○ thirty

Answer Pages

Page 95

Name

Initial Three-Letter Clusters: *scr, str, thr, spr, spl, squ*

Look at each picture below. Listen carefully for the initial consonant cluster. Fill in the missing letters in the word below the picture.

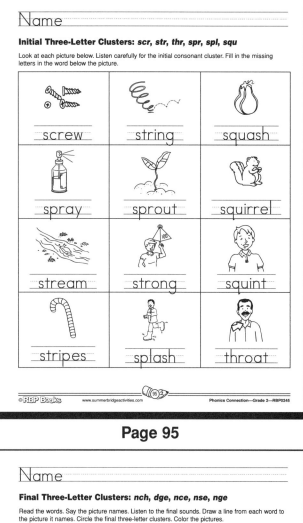

screw | string | squash
spray | sprout | squirrel
stream | strong | squint
stripes | splash | throat

©RBP Books   www.summerbridgeactivities.com   Phonics Connection—Grade 2—RBP0245

Page 95

Page 96

Name

Initial Three-Letter Clusters: *scr, str, thr, spr, spl, sch, squ*

Read the story below. Say each word. Listen carefully for the three-letter clusters. Draw a line under each word with three-letter cluster. Write your favorites in the word bank. Add to or color the picture.

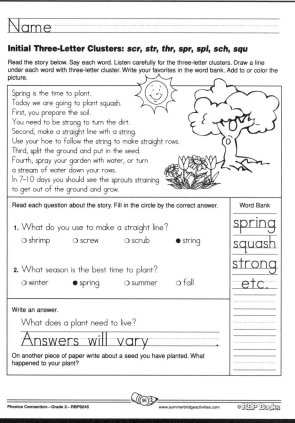

Spring is the time to plant.
Today we are going to plant squash.
First, you prepare the soil.
You need to be strong to turn the dirt.
Second, make a straight line with a string.
Use your hoe to follow the string to make straight rows.
Third, split the ground and put in the seed.
Fourth, spray your garden with water, or turn a stream of water down your rows.
In 7-10 days you should see the sprouts straining to get out of the ground and grow.

Read each question about the story. Fill in the circle by the correct answer.

Word Bank
spring
squash
strong
etc.

1. What do you use to make a straight line?
○ shrimp   ○ screw   ○ scrub   ● string

2. What season is the best time to plant?
○ winter   ● spring   ○ summer   ○ fall

Write an answer.
What does a plant need to live?
Answers will vary.

On another piece of paper write about a seed you have planted. What happened to your plant?

Phonics Connection—Grade 2—RBP0245   www.summerbridgeactivities.com   ©RBP Books

Page 96

Page 97

Name

Final Three-Letter Clusters: *nch, dge, nce, nse, nge*

Read the words. Say the picture names. Listen to the final sounds. Draw a line from each word to the picture it names. Circle the final three-letter clusters. Color the pictures.

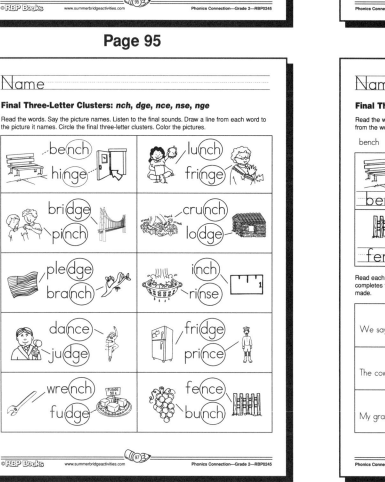

be(nch) / hi(nge)
lu(nch) / fri(nge)
bri(dge) / pi(nch)
cru(nch) / lo(dge)
ple(dge) / bra(nch)
i(nch) / ri(nse)
da(nce) / ju(dge)
fri(dge) / pri(nce)
wre(nch) / fu(dge)
fe(nce) / bu(nch)

©RBP Books   www.summerbridgeactivities.com   Phonics Connection—Grade 2—RBP0245

Page 97

Page 98

Name

Final Three-Letter Clusters: *nch, dge, nce, nse*

Read the words. Say each picture name. Listen for the final three-letter clusters. Write the word from the word list. Color the picture.

bench   pledge   prince   rinse   inch   fudge   fence   lunch

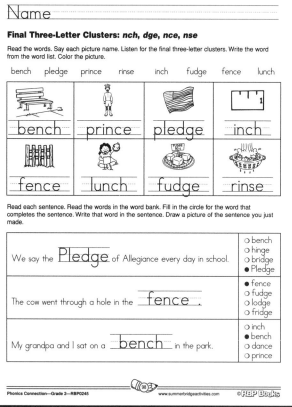

bench | prince | pledge | inch
fence | lunch | fudge | rinse

Read each sentence. Read the words in the word bank. Fill in the circle for the word that completes the sentence. Write that word in the sentence. Draw a picture of the sentence you just made.

We say the **Pledge** of Allegiance every day in school.	○ bench ○ hinge ○ bridge ● Pledge
The cow went through a hole in the **fence**.	● fence ○ fudge ○ lodge ○ fridge
My grandpa and I sat on a **bench** in the park.	○ inch ● bench ○ dance ○ prince

Phonics Connection—Grade 2—RBP0245   www.summerbridgeactivities.com   ©RBP Books

Page 98

Phonics Connection—Grade 2—RBP0245   www.summerbridgeactivities.com   ©RBP Books

Page 99

Name

Final Three-Letter Clusters: *nch, dge, nce, nse, nge*

Look at each picture below. Listen carefully for the three-letter clusters. Fill in the missing letters in the word below the picture.

bench	hinge	fudge
bridge	pinch	lunch
fringe	pledge	branch
dance	inch	fridge

Page 100

Name

Final Three-Letter Clusters: *nch, dge, nce, nse, nge*

Read the story below. Listen carefully for the final clusters. Draw a line under each word with a three-letter cluster. Write your favorites in the word bank. Add to or color the picture.

My grandma is a <u>judge</u>.
Today she took me to see her work.
After work, we went to the park.
We sat on a <u>bench</u>.
She told me stories about a <u>prince</u>.
We watched people go past.
A group came over and talked
Grandma into doing a <u>dance</u>.
Grandma bought us each a glass of <u>punch</u>.
Then it was time to go home for <u>lunch</u>.

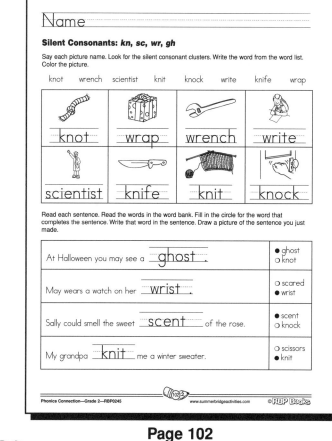

Read each question about the story. Fill in the circle by the correct answer.

Word Bank
judge
bench
prince
dance
punch
lunch

1. In the story what kind of job does Grandma have?
   ○ fudge maker   ● judge   ○ dancer   ○ prince

2. What did Grandma buy to drink?
   ○ water   ○ soda   ○ milk   ● punch

Write an answer.
   What were some of the things they did in the park?
   Answers will vary.

On another piece of paper write about a time you went to the park. Whom did you go with? What did you see and do?

Page 101

Name

Silent Consonants; *kn, sc, wr, gh*

Read the words. Say the picture names. Draw a line from each word to the picture it names. Circle the silent consonant clusters. Color the pictures.

Examples:
The letter *k* can be silent when followed by *n*. The letter *w* can be silent when followed by *r*. The letter *c* can be silent when it follows *s*. The letter *h* can be silent when it follows *g*.

(k)nee   (wr)ist   (sc)issors

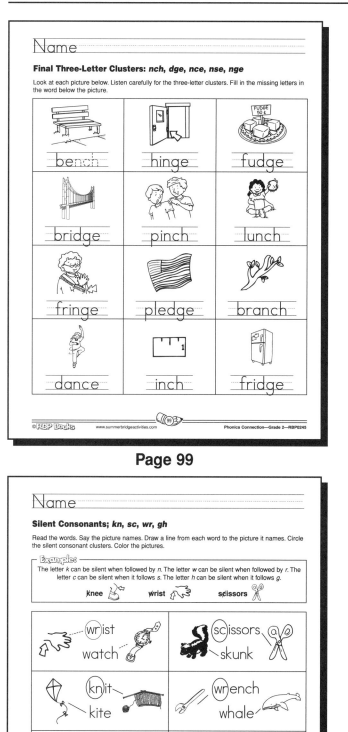

(wr)ist — watch	(sc)issors — skunk
(kn)it — kite	(wr)ench — whale
(gh)ost — goat	(kn)ot — key
(kn)ock — kitten	(sc)ent — snake

Page 102

Name

Silent Consonants: *kn, sc, wr, gh*

Say each picture name. Look for the silent consonant clusters. Write the word from the word list. Color the picture.

knot   wrench   scientist   knit   knock   write   knife   wrap

knot	wrap	wrench	write
scientist	knife	knit	knock

Read each sentence. Read the words in the word bank. Fill in the circle for the word that completes the sentence. Write that word in the sentence. Draw a picture of the sentence you just made.

At Halloween you may see a **ghost**.	● ghost ○ knot
May wears a watch on her **wrist**.	○ scared ● wrist
Sally could smell the sweet **scent** of the rose.	● scent ○ knock
My grandpa **knit** me a winter sweater.	○ scissors ● knit

Answer Pages

Page 103

Name

Silent Consonants: *dg, gh, mb, ck*

Read the words. Say the picture names. Draw a line from each word to the picture it names. Circle the silent consonants. Color the pictures.

Example:

The letter *d* can be silent when followed by *g*. The letter *b* can be silent when followed by *m*. The letter *c* can be silent when it follows *s*. The letter *c* can be silent when followed by a *k*. The letters *gh* together can be silent when followed by *t*.

fu(dg)e   lam(b)   li(gh)t   du(ck)

co(mb)
ei(gh)t

la(mb)
ni(gh)t

ju(dg)e
li(gh)t

thu(mb)
chi(ck)

kni(gh)t
du(ck)

ti(gh)t
lo(ck)

che(ck)
ba(dg)e

clo(ck)
li(mb)

Page 104

Name

Silent Consonants: *dg, gh, mb, ck*

Read the words. Say each picture name. Look for the silent consonant. Write the word from the word list. Color the picture.

judge   limb   night   truck   badge   light   duck   check

| judge | truck | check ✓ | duck |
| light | badge | night | limb |

Read each sentence. Read the words in the word bank. Fill in the circle for the word that completes the sentence. Write that word in the sentence. Draw a picture of the sentence you just made.

The lizard was on the __rock__.	● rock ○ comb
Bats come out and fly at __night__.	● night ○ duck
The sheep can not find her __lamb__.	○ chick ● lamb
We saw eight ducks cross a __bridge__.	● bridge ○ light

Page 105

Name

Silent Consonants:

Read the story below. Say each word. Listen carefully to the sounds. Draw a line under each word with silent consonants. Write your favorites in the word bank. Add to or color the picture.

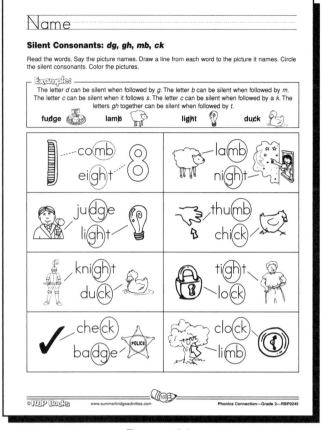

It was Halloween.
Megan knew she was going to be a ghost.
Megan could not wait to knock on all the doors
and say "trick or treat"! Megan was waiting for Mary.
No doubt Mary was going to be
Mary who had a little lamb.
Mary always brought her lamb along.
Megan thought it was wrong to bring the lamb.
The lamb would wrap them up in its rope, tripping them.
Megan went to answer the door.
What a surprise! Mary was a ghastly monster!

Read each question about the story. Fill in the circle by the correct answer.

1. What does *ghastly* mean?
○ a thing that needs gas   ● something very scary

2. What costume was Megan going to wear?
○ lamb   ○ robot   ● ghost   ○ scientist

Write an answer.
What was your favorite costume for Halloween?
__Answers will vary__

On another piece of paper write about your favorite Halloween. Did a friend go with you?

Word Bank
ghost
knock
lamb
etc.

Page 106

Name

Vowels with r: *ar, or*

Read the words. Say the picture names. Draw a line from each word to the picture it names. Circle the vowel with r. Color the pictures.

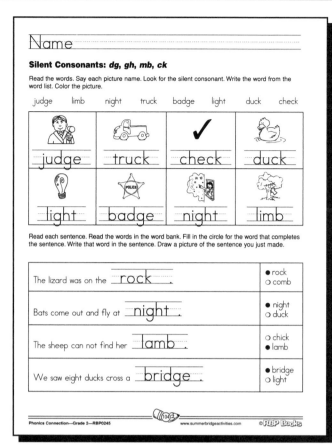

h(ar)p
c(or)n

(ar)m
sw(or)d

p(ar)k
h(or)n

j(ar)
st(or)k

d(ar)t
st(or)m

st(ar)
sn(or)e

y(ar)n
f(or)t

c(ar)
h(or)se

Answer Pages

Page 107

Name

Vowels with r: ar, or

Read the words. Say each picture name. Listen for the vowel with r. Write the word from the word list. Color the picture.

shark   yard   cart   horn   yarn   thorn   dart   torch

| shark | cart | thorn | yard |
| yarn | dart | torch | horn |

Read each sentence. Read the words in the word bank. Fill in the circle for the word that completes the sentence. Write that word in the sentence. Draw a picture of the sentence you just made.

Mark will see a __shark__ in the ocean.	● shark ○ horse
Bert likes to play __darts__.	● darts ○ stork
Grandpa picks __corn__ on the farm.	○ yarn ● corn
My Dad has a very loud __snore__.	○ park ● snore

Page 108

Name

Vowels with r: er, ir, ur

Read the words. Say the picture names. Draw a line from each word to the picture it names. Circle the vowel with r. Color the pictures.

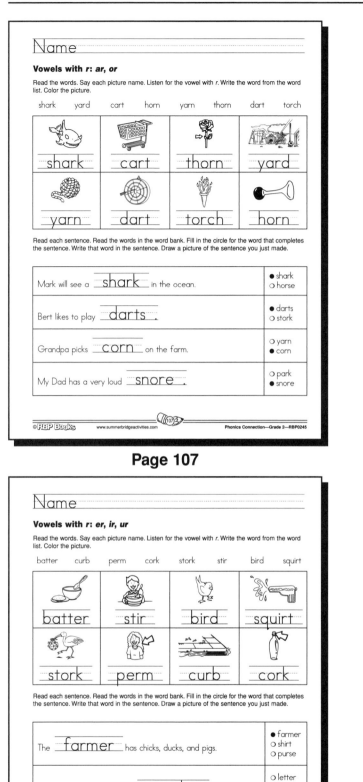

sk(ir)t — nurse
p(er)ch — f(ar)mer
h(er)d — st(ir)
h(ur)t — sh(ir)t
s(ur)f — teach(er)
lett(er) — p(ur)se
j(er)k — g(ir)l
g(er)m — c(ur)l

Page 109

Name

Vowels with r: er, ir, ur

Read the words. Say each picture name. Listen for the vowel with r. Write the word from the word list. Color the picture.

batter   curb   perm   cork   stork   stir   bird   squirt

| batter | stir | bird | squirt |
| stork | perm | curb | cork |

Read each sentence. Read the words in the word bank. Fill in the circle for the word that completes the sentence. Write that word in the sentence. Draw a picture of the sentence you just made.

The __farmer__ has chicks, ducks, and pigs.	● farmer ○ shirt ○ purse
The blue bird can sit on the __perch__.	○ letter ● perch ○ jerk
The __nurse__ can help you get well.	○ her ○ stir ● nurse

Page 110

Name

Vowels with r: er, ir, ur, ar, or

Read the story below. Say each word. Listen carefully for vowels with the r sound. Draw a line under each word with a vowel with an r sound. Write your favorites in the word bank. Add to or color the picture.

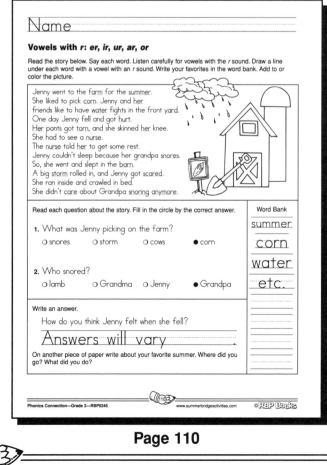

Jenny went to the farm for the summer. She liked to pick corn. Jenny and her friends like to have water fights in the front yard. One day Jenny fell and got hurt. Her pants got torn, and she skinned her knee. She had to see a nurse. The nurse told her to get some rest. Jenny couldn't sleep because her grandpa snores. So, she went and slept in the barn. A big storm rolled in, and Jenny got scared. She ran inside and crawled in bed. She didn't care about Grandpa snoring anymore.

Read each question about the story. Fill in the circle by the correct answer.

1. What was Jenny picking on the farm?
○ snores   ○ storm   ○ cows   ● corn

2. Who snored?
○ lamb   ○ Grandma   ○ Jenny   ● Grandpa

Write an answer.

How do you think Jenny felt when she fell?

Answers will vary

On another piece of paper write about your favorite summer. Where did you go? What did you do?

Word Bank
summer
corn
water
etc.

Answer Pages

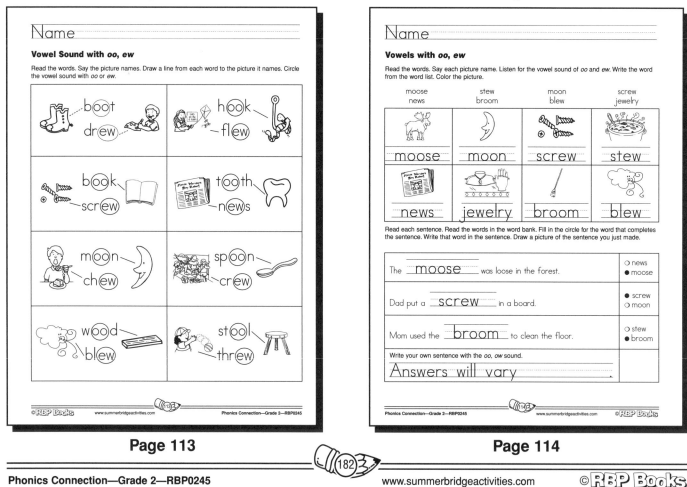
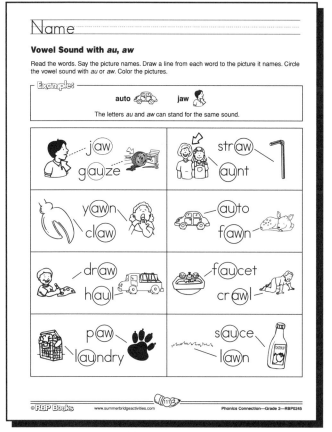

Page 111

Name

Vowel Sound with *au, aw*

Read the words. Say the picture names. Draw a line from each word to the picture it names. Circle the vowel sound with *au* or *aw*. Color the pictures.

Examples:

auto 🚗   jaw 👤

The letters *au* and *aw* can stand for the same sound.

j(aw)
g(au)ze

str(aw)
(au)nt

y(aw)n
cl(aw)

(au)to
f(aw)n

dr(aw)
h(au)l

f(au)cet
cr(aw)l

p(aw)
l(au)ndry

s(au)ce
l(aw)n

Page 112

Name

Vowel Sound with *au, aw*

Read the words. Say each picture name. Listen for the vowel sound of *au* and *aw*. Write the word from the word list. Color the picture.

| autumn | laundry | daughter | shawl |
| claw | draw | jaw | sauce |

autumn   daughter   shawl   laundry

jaw   claw   draw   sauce

Read each sentence. Read the words in the word bank. Fill in the circle for the word that completes the sentence. Write that word in the sentence. Draw a picture of the sentence you just made.

The __hawk__ soared high in the sky.
○ laundry ● hawk

I like to __draw__.
○ gauze ● draw

Water comes out of the __faucet__.
● faucet ○ paw

Write your own sentence with the *au, aw* sound.
__Answers will vary__

Page 113

Name

Vowel Sound with *oo, ew*

Read the words. Say the picture names. Draw a line from each word to the picture it names. Circle the vowel sound with *oo* or *ew*.

b(oo)t
dr(ew)

h(oo)k
fl(ew)

b(oo)k
scr(ew)

t(oo)th
n(ew)s

m(oo)n
ch(ew)

sp(oo)n
cr(ew)

w(oo)d
bl(ew)

st(oo)l
thr(ew)

Page 114

Name

Vowels with *oo, ew*

Read the words. Say each picture name. Listen for the vowel sound of *oo* and *ew*. Write the word from the word list. Color the picture.

| moose | stew | moon | screw |
| news | broom | blew | jewelry |

moose   moon   screw   stew

news   jewelry   broom   blew

Read each sentence. Read the words in the word bank. Fill in the circle for the word that completes the sentence. Write that word in the sentence. Draw a picture of the sentence you just made.

The __moose__ was loose in the forest.
○ news ● moose

Dad put a __screw__ in a board.
● screw ○ moon

Mom used the __broom__ to clean the floor.
○ stew ● broom

Write your own sentence with the *oo, ow* sound.
__Answers will vary__

Answer Pages

Page 115

Name

Vowels with *au*, *aw*, *oo* and *ew*

Read the story below. Say each word. Listen carefully for the *au*, *aw*, *oo*, and *ew* sounds. Draw a line under each word with *au*, *aw*, *oo*, *ew* sound. Write your favorites in the word bank. Add to or color the picture.

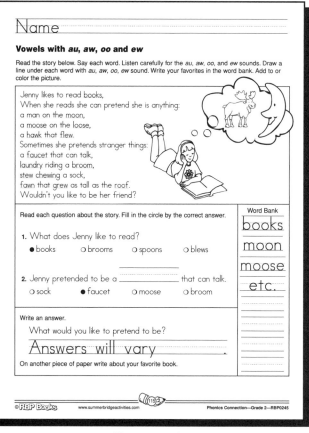

Jenny likes to read books,
When she reads she can pretend she is anything:
a man on the moon,
a moose on the loose,
a hawk that flew.
Sometimes she pretends stranger things:
a faucet that can talk,
laundry riding a broom,
stew chewing a sock,
fawn that grew as tall as the roof.
Wouldn't you like to be her friend?

Read each question about the story. Fill in the circle by the correct answer.

1. What does Jenny like to read?
   ● books   ○ brooms   ○ spoons   ○ blews

2. Jenny pretended to be a _____ that can talk.
   ○ sock   ● faucet   ○ moose   ○ broom

Word Bank
books
moon
moose
etc.

Write an answer.
What would you like to pretend to be?
Answers will vary

On another piece of paper write about your favorite book.

Page 116

Name

Diphthongs: *ou*, *oi*, *oy*, *ow*

Read the words. Say the picture names. Draw a line from each word to the picture it names. Circle the vowel sound with *ou*, *oi*, *oy*, or *ow*. Color the pictures.

Examples:
The sound in the middle of *coin* is spelled by the letters *oi*. The sound in the middle of *toys* is spelled by the letters *oy*.
The sound in the middle of *mouse* is spelled by the letters *ou*. The sound at the end of *cow* is spelled by the letters *ow*.

b(o)y
m(ou)ntain

s(oi)l
fl(ow)er

t(oy)
cl(ow)n

b(oi)l
m(ou)th

j(oy)
cl(ou)d

c(oi)n
c(ow)

R(oy)
t(ow)el

n(oi)se
c(ou)ch

Page 117

Name

Diphthongs: *ou*, *oi*, *oy*, *ow*

Read the words. Say each picture name. Listen for the vowel sounds *ou*, *oi*, *oy*, and *ow*. Write the word from the word list. Color the picture.

gown / coin   oyster / mouse   plow / soil   boy / mountain

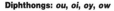

gown   soil   mouse   coin

mountain   boy   plow   oyster

Read each sentence. Read the words in the word bank. Fill in the circle for the word that completes the sentence. Write that word in the sentence. Draw a picture of the sentence you just made.

We went downtown to see the clown .	● clown ○ towel
Nancy has a noisy toy .	○ ploy ● toy
The mouse ran into the house .	● house ○ coin
Write your own sentence with the *ou*, *oi*, *oy*, or *ow* sounds. Answers will vary .	

Page 118

Name

Diphthongs: *ou*, *oi*, *oy*, *ow*

Read the story below. Say each word. Listen carefully for the sounds. Draw a line under each word with *ou*, *oi*, *oy*, or *ow*. Write your favorites in the word bank. Add to or color the picture.

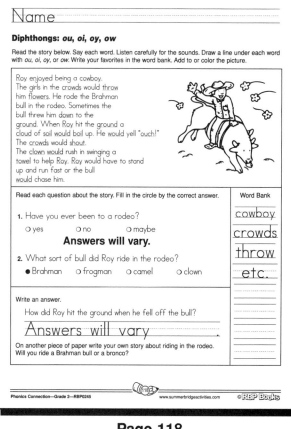

Roy enjoyed being a cowboy.
The girls in the crowds would throw
him flowers. He rode the Brahman
bull in the rodeo. Sometimes the
bull threw him down to the
ground. When Roy hit the ground a
cloud of soil would boil up. He would yell "ouch!"
The crowds would shout.
The clown would rush in swinging a
towel to help Roy. Roy would have to stand
up and run fast or the bull
would chase him.

Read each question about the story. Fill in the circle by the correct answer.

1. Have you ever been to a rodeo?
   ○ yes   ○ no   ○ maybe
   Answers will vary.

2. What sort of bull did Roy ride in the rodeo?
   ● Brahman   ○ frogman   ○ camel   ○ clown

Word Bank
cowboy
crowds
throw
etc.

Write an answer.
How did Roy hit the ground when he fell off the bull?
Answers will vary

On another piece of paper write your own story about riding in the rodeo. Will you ride a Brahman bull or a bronco?

Answer Pages

Name

Root Words Ending with -ed, -ing

Read the words. Say the picture names. Add -ed or -ing to the root word. Color the pictures.

When a root word ends with one vowel followed by a consonant, double the consonant before adding -ed or -ing.

	bat	batted	batting
	fish	fished	fishing
	paint	painted	painting
	start	started	starting
	toss	tossed	tossing
	help	helped	helping
	rub	rubbed	rubbing
	miss	missed	missing

Page 119

Name

Root Words Ending with -ed, -ing

Read the words. Say the picture names. Add -ed or -ing to the root word. Color the pictures.

When a root word ends with silent e, drop the e before adding -ed or -ing.

	bake	baked	baking
	hike	hiked	hiking
	dance	danced	dancing
	use	used	using
	hope	hoped	hoping
	dine	dined	dining
	carve	carved	carving
	rake	raked	raking

Page 120

Name

Words Ending with -ed, -ing

Read the words. Say the picture names. Add -ed or -ing to the root word. Color the pictures.

When a word ends in a consonant followed by y, change the y to i before adding -ed. When a word ends in a vowel followed by y, just add -ed. Do not change y before adding -ing to a word that ends in y.

	dry	dried	drying
	stay	stayed	staying
	play	played	playing
	hurry	hurried	hurrying
	cry	cried	crying
	study	studied	studying
	carry	carried	carrying
	try	tried	trying

Page 121

Name

Words Ending with -ed, -ing

Read the story below. Listen carefully for -ed and -ing word endings. Circle the correct word to make the sentence complete. Write the **root word** in the word bank. Add to or color the picture.

Linda's teacher (ask , asked, asking) her to do a
worksheet on words ending in −ed and -ing.
She (wish, wished, wishing) that she could visit a far away place instead.
Linda (work, worked, working) on the lesson, but pretty soon she was
(daydream, daydreamed, daydreaming).
Linda became a magician in her dream.
She (pull, pulled, pulling) a rabbit out of her hat.
The rabbit (hop, hopped, hopping) off the stage.

Read each question about the story. Fill in the circle by the correct answer.

1. What did Linda become in her daydream?
   ○ rabbit   ○ teacher   ● magician   ○ student

2. What did Linda pull from her hat?
   ● rabbit   ○ teacher   ○ magician   ○ student

Write an answer.
   What didn't Linda want to do?
   Linda didn't want to do a worksheet.

On another piece of paper write about a magic show. What was your favorite trick?

Root Word Bank

ask

wish

work

daydream

pull

hop

Page 122

Answer Pages

Page 123

Name

Words Ending with -er and -est

Look at the pictures. Read the words. Draw a line from each word to the picture that matches it.

The ending -er sometimes means "more." For example, *smaller* means "more small." The ending -est means "most." For example, *smallest* means "most small."

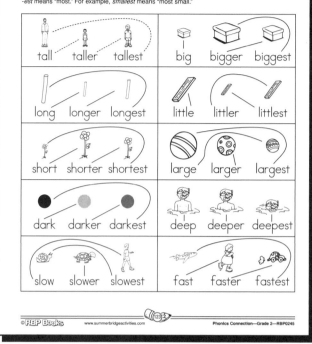

tall   taller   tallest   big   bigger   biggest

long   longer   longest   little   littler   littlest

short   shorter   shortest   large   larger   largest

dark   darker   darkest   deep   deeper   deepest

slow   slower   slowest   fast   faster   fastest

© RBP Books   www.summerbridgeactivities.com   Phonics Connection—Grade 2—RBP0245   123

Page 123

Page 124

Name

Words Endings with -er and -est

Read the words. Say each picture name. Listen for the words ending with -er and -est. Write the word from the word list under the picture. Color the picture.

tallest   deepest   smaller   longest
shorter   larger   faster   older

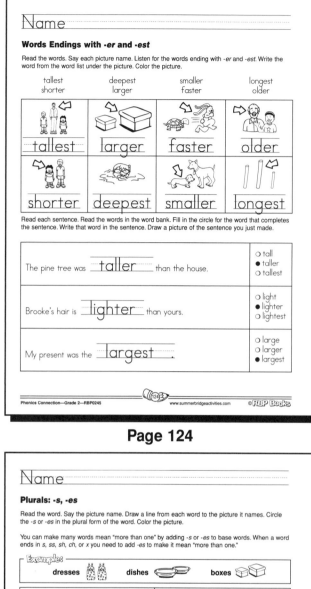

tallest   larger   faster   older

shorter   deepest   smaller   longest

Read each sentence. Read the words in the word bank. Fill in the circle for the word that completes the sentence. Write that word in the sentence. Draw a picture of the sentence you just made.

The pine tree was **taller** than the house.	○ tall ● taller ○ tallest
Brooke's hair is **lighter** than yours.	○ light ● lighter ○ lightest
My present was the **largest**.	○ large ○ larger ● largest

Phonics Connection—Grade 2—RBP0245   www.summerbridgeactivities.com   © RBP Books   124

Page 124

Page 125

Name

Words Ending with -er and -est

Read the story. Listen carefully for -ed and -ing word endings. Circle the correct word to make the sentence complete. Write the **root word** in the word bank. Add to or color the picture.

The (old, older, oldest) lady on the block lived in the (small, smaller, smallest) house. She had the (loud, louder, loudest) dog you ever heard. She had the (sweet, sweeter, sweetest) smelling flowers you ever smelled. Her yellow blouse was so (bright, brighter, brightest) you could lose your sight. Her homemade stew was (tasty, tastier, tastiest) than most. Her old hands were (rough, rougher, roughest), and her touch was scratchy. She was the (nice, nicer, nicest) old lady on the block.

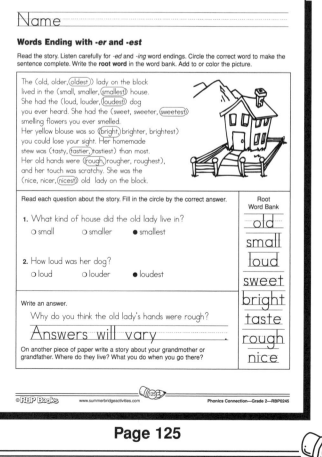

Read each question about the story. Fill in the circle by the correct answer.

1. What kind of house did the old lady live in?
   ○ small   ○ smaller   ● smallest

2. How loud was her dog?
   ○ loud   ○ louder   ● loudest

Write an answer.
   Why do you think the old lady's hands were rough?
   Answers will vary

On another piece of paper write a story about your grandmother or grandfather. Where do they live? What you do when you go there?

Root Word Bank
old
small
loud
sweet
bright
taste
rough
nice

© RBP Books   www.summerbridgeactivities.com   Phonics Connection—Grade 2—RBP0245   125

Page 125

Page 126

Name

Plurals: -s, -es

Read the word. Say the picture name. Draw a line from each word to the picture it names. Circle the -s or -es in the plural form of the word. Color the picture.

You can make many words mean "more than one" by adding -s or -es to base words. When a word ends in s, ss, sh, ch, or x you need to add -es to make it mean "more than one."

Examples: dresses   dishes   boxes

bird   birds   lid   lids

jet   jets   bus   buses

peach   peaches   pine   pines

hand   hands   cake   cakes

Phonics Connection—Grade 2—RBP0245   www.summerbridgeactivities.com   © RBP Books   126

Page 126

Answer Pages

Page 127

Plurals: -s, -es

Read the words. Say each picture name. Make each word plural by adding -s or -es. Color the picture.

| cap | hut | top | pig |
| cube | kite | rope | cake |

| caps | cubes | huts | ropes |
| pigs | cakes | tops | kites |

Read each sentence. Read the words in the word bank. Fill in the circle for the word that completes the sentence. Write that word in the sentence. Draw a picture of the sentence you just made.

Matt likes to eat __peaches__ .	○ peach ● peaches
Three __ducks__ went swimming.	○ duck ● ducks
I washed both of my __hands__ .	● hands ○ hand
I missed the school __bus__ .	● bus ○ buses

Page 127

Page 128

Plurals: -s, -es, -ies

Read the word. Say the picture name. Draw a line from each word to the picture it names. Circle the -s, -es or -ies in the plural form of the word. Color the picture.

When a word ends in a consonant followed by a y, change the y to i and add -es to make it mean "more than one." When a word ends in a vowel followed by y, just add -s.

Examples:

| story stories | boy boys |

baby / babies	book / book(s)
key / key(s)	watch / watch(es)
pony / pon(ies)	frog / frog(s)
bunny / bunn(ies)	daisy / dais(ies)

Page 128

Page 129

Plurals: -s, -es, -ies

Read the words. Say each picture name. Make each word plural by adding -s or -ies. Write the word from the word list under the picture. Color the picture.

| story | penny | baby | tray |
| bunny | boy | pony | daisy |

| stories | boys | babies | pennies |
| ponies | daisies | trays | bunnies |

Read each sentence. Read the words in the word bank. Fill in the circle for the word that completes the sentence. Write that word in the sentence. Draw a picture of the sentence you just made.

The __babies__ were crying all night long.	○ baby ● babies
The __bunnies__ were hopping in the field.	○ bunny ● bunnies
Four __boys__ joined a band.	○ boy ● boys
My mom gave me ten __pennies__ .	○ penny ● pennies

Page 129

Page 130

Plurals: -s, -es

Read the story. Underline the words in plural form. Write the root word in the word bank. Add to or color the picture.

Frogs live almost everywhere. Frogs live in ponds, marshes and ditches. The largest frog is eight inches long and weighs one and one half pounds. They come in many colors: green, yellow, blue, and red. Frogs eat insects like flies. Frog babies are tadpoles. The babies use gills to breathe. During their first ten weeks they grow legs and lungs and lose their tails. Then, they hop on land and start croaking. Their chorus of croaks sounds like motorcycles roaring.

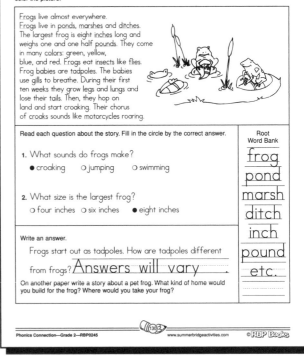

Read each question about the story. Fill in the circle by the correct answer.

1. What sounds do frogs make?
   ● croaking ○ jumping ○ swimming

2. What size is the largest frog?
   ○ four inches ○ six inches ● eight inches

Write an answer.
Frogs start out as tadpoles. How are tadpoles different from frogs? __Answers will vary__ .

On another paper write a story about a pet frog. What kind of home would you build for the frog? Where would you take your frog?

Root Word Bank

frog
pond
marsh
ditch
inch
pound
etc.

Page 130

Answer Pages

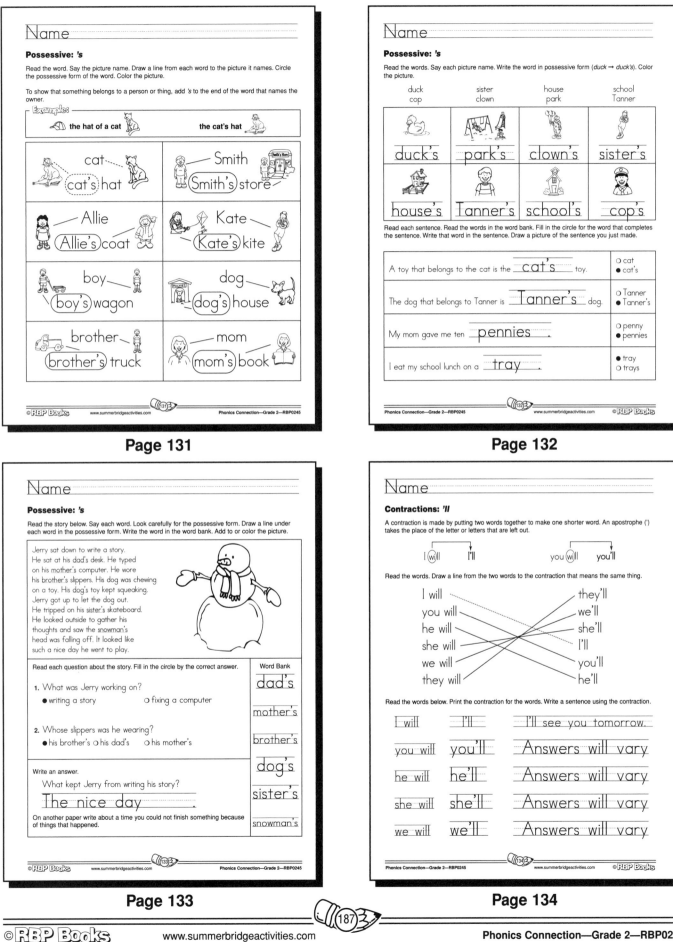

Page 131

Possessive: 's

Read the word. Say the picture name. Draw a line from each word to the picture it names. Circle the possessive form of the word. Color the picture.

To show that something belongs to a person or thing, add 's to the end of the word that names the owner.

Examples:
| the hat of a cat | the cat's hat |

cat — cat's hat
Smith — Smith's store
Allie — Allie's coat
Kate — Kate's kite
boy — boy's wagon
dog — dog's house
brother — brother's truck
mom — mom's book

Page 132

Possessive: 's

Read the words. Say each picture name. Write the word in possessive form (duck → duck's). Color the picture.

duck cop | sister clown | house park | school Tanner

duck's | park's | clown's | sister's
house's | Tanner's | school's | cop's

Read each sentence. Read the words in the word bank. Fill in the circle for the word that completes the sentence. Write that word in the sentence. Draw a picture of the sentence you just made.

A toy that belongs to the cat is the ___cat's___ toy.	○ cat ● cat's
The dog that belongs to Tanner is ___Tanner's___ dog.	○ Tanner ● Tanner's
My mom gave me ten ___pennies___.	○ penny ● pennies
I eat my school lunch on a ___tray___.	● tray ○ trays

Page 133

Possessive: 's

Read the story below. Say each word. Look carefully for the possessive form. Draw a line under each word in the possessive form. Write the word in the word bank. Add to or color the picture.

Jerry sat down to write a story. He sat at his dad's desk. He typed on his mother's computer. He wore his brother's slippers. His dog was chewing on a toy. His dog's toy kept squeaking. Jerry got up to let the dog out. He tripped on his sister's skateboard. He looked outside to gather his thoughts and saw the snowman's head was falling off. It looked like such a nice day he went to play.

Read each question about the story. Fill in the circle by the correct answer.

Word Bank
dad's
mother's
brother's
dog's
sister's
snowman's

1. What was Jerry working on?
● writing a story   ○ fixing a computer

2. Whose slippers was he wearing?
● his brother's   ○ his dad's   ○ his mother's

Write an answer.
What kept Jerry from writing his story?
The nice day

On another paper write about a time you could not finish something because of things that happened.

Page 134

Contractions: 'll

A contraction is made by putting two words together to make one shorter word. An apostrophe (') takes the place of the letter or letters that are left out.

I will → I'll   you will → you'll

Read the words. Draw a line from the two words to the contraction that means the same thing.

I will   they'll
you will   we'll
he will   she'll
she will   I'll
we will   you'll
they will   he'll

Read the words below. Print the contraction for the words. Write a sentence using the contraction.

I will	I'll	I'll see you tomorrow.
you will	you'll	Answers will vary
he will	he'll	Answers will vary
she will	she'll	Answers will vary
we will	we'll	Answers will vary

Answer Pages

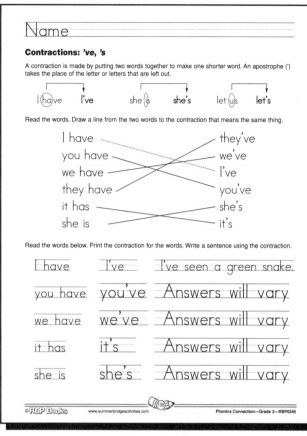

Page 135

Contractions: 've, 's

A contraction is made by putting two words together to make one shorter word. An apostrophe (') takes the place of the letter or letters that are left out.

I ha(ve) → **I've**   she (is) → **she's**   let (us) → **let's**

Read the words. Draw a line from the two words to the contraction that means the same thing.

I have	they've
you have	we've
we have	I've
they have	you've
it has	she's
she is	it's

Read the words below. Print the contraction for the words. Write a sentence using the contraction.

I have	I've	I've seen a green snake.
you have	you've	Answers will vary
we have	we've	Answers will vary
it has	it's	Answers will vary
she is	she's	Answers will vary

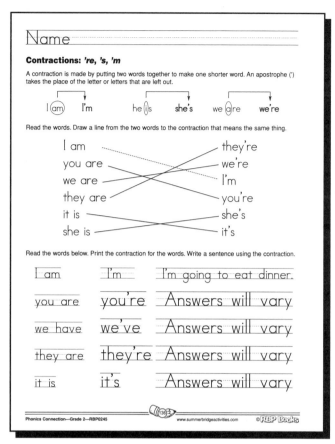

Page 136

Contractions: 're, 's, 'm

A contraction is made by putting two words together to make one shorter word. An apostrophe (') takes the place of the letter or letters that are left out.

I (am) → **I'm**   he (is) → **she's**   we (are) → **we're**

Read the words. Draw a line from the two words to the contraction that means the same thing.

I am	they're
you are	we're
we are	I'm
they are	you're
it is	she's
she is	it's

Read the words below. Print the contraction for the words. Write a sentence using the contraction.

I am	I'm	I'm going to eat dinner.
you are	you're	Answers will vary
we have	we've	Answers will vary
they are	they're	Answers will vary
it is	it's	Answers will vary

Page 137

Contractions: 't

A contraction is made by putting two words together to make one shorter word. An apostrophe (') takes the place of the letter or letters that are left out.

has n(o)t → **hasn't**   could n(o)t → **couldn't**

Read the words. Draw a line from the words to the contraction that means the same thing.

have not	hasn't	cannot	shouldn't
has not	hadn't	could not	can't
had not	haven't	should not	couldn't

do not	didn't	is not	aren't
did not	doesn't	are not	wasn't
does not	don't	was not	isn't

Read the contractions below. Print the words. Write a sentence using the contraction.

haven't	have	not	I haven't read the book.
weren't	were	not	Answers will vary
didn't	did	not	Answers will vary
isn't	is	not	Answers will vary
won't	will	not	Answers will vary

Page 138

Contractions

Read the letter. Say each word. Listen carefully for contractions. Write the contraction for the two words on the line above the words.

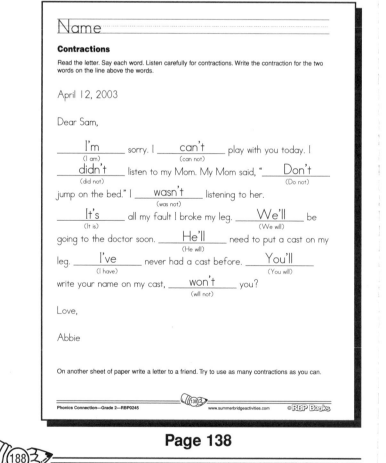

April 12, 2003

Dear Sam,

__I'm__ (I am) sorry. I __can't__ (can not) play with you today. I __didn't__ (did not) listen to my Mom. My Mom said, "__Don't__ (Do not) jump on the bed." I __wasn't__ (was not) listening to her. __It's__ (It is) all my fault I broke my leg. __We'll__ (We will) be going to the doctor soon. __He'll__ (He will) need to put a cast on my leg. __I've__ (I have) never had a cast before. __You'll__ (You will) write your name on my cast, __won't__ (will not) you?

Love,

Abbie

On another sheet of paper write a letter to a friend. Try to use as many contractions as you can.